ARCHETYPAL IMAGERY
AND THE SPIRITUAL SELF

of related interest

Shamanism and Spirituality in
Therapeutic Practice
An Introduction
Christa Mackinnon
ISBN 978 1 84819 081 8
eISBN 978 0 85701 068 1

How to Incorporate Wellness Coaching
into Your Therapeutic Practice
A Handbook for Therapists and Counsellors
Laurel Alexander
ISBN 978 1 84819 063 4
eISBN 978 0 85701 034 6

How to Give Clients the Skills
to Stop Panic Attacks
Don't Forget to Breathe
Sandra Scheinbaum
ISBN 978 1 84905 887 2
eISBN 978 0 85700 603 5

Inner Dialogue In Daily Life
Contemporary Approaches to Personal and
Professional Development in Psychotherapy
Edited by Charles Eigen
ISBN 978 1 84905 983 1
eISBN 978 0 85700 896 1

Dramatherapy with Myth and Fairytale
The Golden Stories of Sesame
Jenny Pearson, Mary Smail and Pat Watts
Foreword by Alida Gersie
Illustrated by Camilla Jessel
ISBN 978 1 84905 030 2
eISBN 978 0 85700 438 3

ARCHETYPAL
IMAGERY
and the
SPIRITUAL
SELF

Techniques for Coaches and Therapists

ANNABELLE NELSON

SINGING
DRAGON

LONDON AND PHILADELPHIA

First published in 2014
by Singing Dragon
an imprint of Jessica Kingsley Publishers
73 Collier Street
London N1 9BE, UK
and
400 Market Street, Suite 400
Philadelphia, PA 19106, USA

www.singingdragon.com

Library of Congress Cataloging in Publication Data
Nelson, Annabelle, author.
  Archetypal Imagery and the Spiritual Self: Techniques for Coaches and Therapists /
Annabelle Nelson.
  Includes bibliographical references and index.
  ISBN 978-1-84819-220-1 (alk. paper)
  I. Title.
  [DNLM: 1. Imagery (Psychotherapy)--methods. 2. Spiritual Therapies--methods. WM
420.5.I3]
  RC489.P72
  616.89'14--dc23
                          2013049416

British Library Cataloguing in Publication Data
A CIP catalogue record for this book is available from the British Library

ISBN 978 1 84819 220 1
eISBN 978 0 85701 169 5

Printed and bound in Great Britain

For McCoy, Jody and Sage,
the most beautiful people in my world

ACKNOWLEDGMENTS

I would like to thank Fielding Graduate University for many things including giving me sabbaticals to work on the book, providing sessions I could use to test concepts, awarding me travel expenses to go to conferences and for graduate students who helped immeasurably in the development of this work. Particular thanks are extended to B.B., A.P. and D.K. Thanks also go to Takeshi Matsui for teaching me how to do imagery in the body at an imagery conference in Fukuoka, Japan, 1988. The book would not have happened without visions from spiritual entities including Sophia, Vajrasattva, Ganesha, Krishna and others. My family deserves thanks for loyalty, encouragement, fun and for always being proud of me. My sister Linda gets praise for calling me daily. I want to honor my parents for teaching me at the age of five that I was going to graduate school, and encouraging me to go beyond my limits. I've always been thankful for the opportunities which my education affords. I also wish to thank the psychologists' shoulders on which I stand. In addition, I am filled with gratitude for the many settings which have encouraged my creativity, theory-building and writing. These include wilderness, libraries, classrooms and sacred sites in India, Turkey, Japan and Guatemala. On a practical note, Lori Garcia of TLC Unlimited needs recognition as one of the most amazing graphic artists I know. Finally, I also wish to thank Lisa Clark, Senior Commissioning Editor for Jessica Kingsley Publishers, for her support and enthusiasm for this project.

CONTENTS

INTRODUCTION

People come to coaching or therapy for many reasons which include emotional distress, problem solving or professional guidance, and increasingly they are interested in spirituality. Coaches and therapists working with these clients will find that this book is designed especially for them. Using the natural psychodynamic of archetype imagination, I've created a practical model that combines psychological health and spiritual awareness to help clients move to wisdom. The roots to my model were planted a long time ago.

I am a psychology professor at a graduate university, and one of my colleagues used to say, "We all think we know so many things, but really we all just have one book in us." This is my one book, and I've been developing the concepts for 40 years. When I was a graduate student, I did research at a special needs preschool in the morning and in the afternoon I taught undergraduate statistics, besides doing my own research. I operated in what can only be described as a manic state, running from one activity to another. At one point, I noticed that I was lighted-headed from bending up and down all morning for preschoolers. To compensate, I spaced out on TV in the afternoons after teaching. Of course as an intellectual I judged myself for watching TV, so I was watching PBS, and Lilias the yoga teacher appeared. At a certain point, I just started doing yoga while watching her show. I made fun of her initially, since she was a bit saccharine. But finally, I thought, "Why not?" Surprisingly it had an immediate effect on me. My mind became more open and spacious, and I had room to be aware of what was happening inside and outside of my limited perception. This experience from over 35 years ago has motivated my quest to document and transmit practical techniques to create open minds to tap inner potential.

There have many twists and turns on this road, from doing yoga with children, researching imagery, working with Native American tribes, teaching in India, becoming a master storyteller and creating a theory that blends Carl Jung's (1970) theory with Vedantic Hindu philosophy. But always the intent was to learn how to tap inner forces for health and healing, so I could share this with others. Abraham Maslow (1970) called this inner force the actualizing tendency. Carl Rogers (1961) called it the creative force, and in Vedantic philosophy (Vivekananda 1956), it is the *atman* or spiritual Self.[1] This dynamic, health-promoting part of the mind is healing and activates potential. But it was buried in the unconscious, hard to find.

During my imagery research phase, I thought I would become a workshop guru, travel all over the country and make a mint. As a reminder, imagery is thinking in internal sensations, seeing a picture, feeling the self walking, smelling freshly baked bread, and other things like that. I did not become a well-paid guru, but I had a few gigs, and it was fun to delve into the field. I personally did research into using imagery to increase children's creativity (Nelson 1991). I attended imagery workshops in New York and Fukuoka, Japan, and learned about how imagery could change the number of immune cells, or help engineers visualize new technology, or assist the emotional healing of trauma.

During the late 1980s, there was a field called psychoneuroimmunology (Pert 1997), or how thoughts could affect the body's immune response. In 1990, I was slated to do a workshop called *Healing with Imagery* at Phoenix Camelback Hospital, and my intent was to make the unconscious mind a friendly place. One attribute of imagery is that it can travel into the unconscious mind, bypassing the ego. This is quite a feat since the human ego moves uncomfortable emotions, memories and sensations into the unconscious. Because of this it has a vested

---

1   Self is capitalized when it refers to the part of consciousness connected to the energetic domain, in the unconscious.

interest in keeping things locked up. However, the mind needs to open up to access the healing forces hidden away.

Imagery is mediated in the brain by a small rim-like structure underneath the two cerebral cortices, called the limbic system (Pribram 1981). One part of this system, the amygdala, retrieves long-term memories. Another part of the limbic system is the hippocampus, which regulates autonomic nervous system activity. These functions were previously thought to be outside of conscious control, until biofeedback showed that visualization could change blood pressure levels (Achterberg 1985). Thinking in images opens up both memory and autonomic body functions since they all happen in the same place, the limbic system.

My workshop taught nurses and other medical staff to use imagery to assist in relaxation and the actual physiological healing process. Some think that the unconscious is an unfriendly and scary place, and it certainly can be if buried trauma or chaotic emotions erupt. However, if a human has a focus of attention, as happens during imagery, then the unconscious can open safely. I wanted to create a story to show that the unconscious could be a friendly place. To convey this I made up one about a multiple racial woman, Sophia, who lives in a time like the past, but also like the future. She is a book-binder's daughter with a mind of her own. She accepts the challenge of being the "best woman" in the village, only to be surprised that she must be sacrificed to a dragon, ostensibly keeping the village safe. The dragon, named Claude, turns out to be a vegetarian. He is very lonely and talks Sophia into staying with him for ten years exploring deep caves in the earth. Both the dragon and the caves represented the unconscious mind. The dragon is kind and ancient with much wisdom to impart. The caves aren't frightening at all, but turn out to be full of wondrous sculptures in the form of stalactites and shine from the reflections of precious metals and gems in the wall. The archetypes in my story, entitled Sophia and Claude, became the basis for this book's model. Both the cave and the dragon were archetypes that opened the unconscious to bring back healing and insight. Obviously, I've developed many more details and sophistication in the ensuing years, but the core idea has held up.

SPIRITUAL EMERGENCE

There is a spiritual emergence in our culture. It has become a mainstream phenomenon, with ashrams in most metropolitan areas, and yoga taught daily in athletic clubs. People want the experience of sustained joy and peace, and they look to popular spiritual teachers and Eastern practices such as yoga to help them achieve it. No longer is it enough to join a church or attend a service; instead they want an inner spiritual experience. This quest for transcendence has been joined with the psychological pursuit of wellbeing. More than a belief system, people want to change the inner world through yoga or meditation, and also through less mainstream experiences such as shamanic journeys. The idea is to be spiritual and at the same time to have day-to-day happiness. I call this "a yearning for wisdom." Changing the inner world can make this happen.

The cultural phenomenon of merging Eastern spirituality with human potential psychology has been growing since 1920 when a yogi, Paramahansa Yogananda (2005), author of *Autobiography of a Yogi*, came to the International Congress of Religion in Boston. The seeds of his teaching germinated until they sprouted in the 1960s and then bloomed in the 1970s with the human potential movement. About this time, my friends were getting mantras from the Maharishi to do Transcendental Meditation, and listening to Ram Dass (1974) who was touring the country to promote his book, *The Only Dance There Is*. Famous psychologist Fritz Perls (1992) started the Esalen Institute on the California coast, to help people embody human potential. My friends and I talked about being enlightened in one lifetime. There were many words for what we wanted. These included becoming enlightened or zen-like, or spiritual or "high," or even achieving nirvana. But the long and short of it was that we wanted to escape everyday worries and create a consistent inner state of peace and joy. We didn't realize how naïve we were in thinking we could do some yoga or meditate and then be enlightened. My friends and I didn't realize that the task was more difficult than we ever imagined, and the bliss states we found were transient.

Practitioners of yoga and meditation experience highs and bliss, but these states don't seem to last. They end up back in the throes of emotional ups and downs, sometimes in despair and sadness. They struggle with the desire for consistent states and may look to psychology to deal with emotions. There is a contemporary positive approach (Seligman 2002) aimed at helping people create happiness. These two movements of Eastern spiritual practices and psychology are converging (Post and Wade 2009), with a growing sophistication of how the two interrelate to create an awakened awareness for sustained transformation.

The quest in the twenty-first century is unique since it combines the psychology of human potential with the desire to be spiritual. Now we have the gift and opportunity to merge the streams of human capacity of mind, body, spirit and emotions. Psychological and spiritual experiences are intertwined. The person who is psychologically healthy with a durable state of wellbeing is kind and calm, which are descriptors of spirituality. My background as a psychologist, yogi and meditator has given me some hard-won lessons for tracking this integrated path.

WISDOM

I like Chögyam Trungpa's (1991) idea on the goal of human development. He was a Tibetan Rinpoche[2] who started Naropa University in Boulder, Colorado. In his book, *The Heart of the Buddha*, he described what he considered wisdom. If a person is wise then the mind is soft, warm, friendly, joyous and spacious. This sounds right to me to describe what we are all aiming for psychologically and spiritually. A person whose mind has these characteristics would engender peace and joy in others. In essence this person would personify wisdom.

---

2   This designation is for incarnated lamas who are recognized by authorities within a lineage, also known as superior dharma masters.

Over the years I have experienced glimpses of how to transform my mind to Trungpa's spaciousness. During a conference on humanistic psychology in Boston, Massachusetts, I was describing this feeling to a colleague during dinner. As I was telling him about some of my problems, he analyzed me as psychologists are wont to do. This often annoys me, and I was resistant. I told him I was okay.

"But you know, really, everything is good."

He responded, "You're not all right."

"But I am. I can move into the spiritual dimension at any time."

Disbelieving, he asked me to explain. I could sense what I wanted to express to him, but spiritual things are ineffable, and it was hard to find the words. A metaphor popped up in my mind of using a wave to explain what it feels like. I drew it on a napkin and showed how for the most part consciousness goes up and down just like this, as shown in Figure I.1.

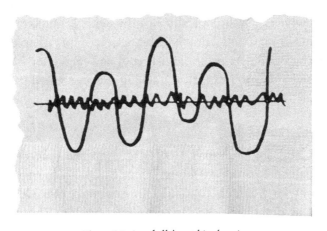

Figure I.1 Annabelle's napkin drawing

Emotions and sensations create wide fluctuations in consciousness from despair to elation. But there is a constant hum connected to the energy field underlying this reality, a focus amidst the gyrations of sensations and thoughts.

I put my finger on the midpoint, half-way between the top and bottom curves. I said, "There is a pulse of energy slightly below the surface of reality which can be sensed. It is constant and rhythmic and is the source of our perceived ups and downs." He looked baffled, but I touched his heart so he could feel the steadiness I was experiencing. A little embarrassed by this spontaneous demonstration, I took my hand away quickly. But he asked me to return my hand. Then he said he felt what I was talking about.

After I explained this to him, I remembered a metaphor from Taoism. The Tao has light on one side containing a dark circle, dark on the other side containing a light circle, with a curving line between. As in the drawing shown in Figure I.2, there is a place in the middle of the opposites that is constant. However, if this became animated, it would vibrate gently. Creating space allows the opposites to coexist, so that one can sense this in-between space, underlying opposites, such as light–dark, anger–calm, love–hate, male–female or human–spiritual. This is the hum of creation, and the wise mind can be open to it.

Figure I.2 The Tao, symbolizing "the way", which is the energy field that underlies reality

As one transforms the inner world to wisdom, one can "sense" the Tao. All human activity can gain energy by aligning with the Tao or the forces of creation.

To create this change one follows a path, but there is no end, just as in psychologist Carl Rogers' quote, "Life is a journey, not a destination." The spiritual seeker does not really go anywhere, arrive anywhere or achieve a higher state. Rather, the person changes from the inside out in the here and now.

It is an effable concept, but there is hope. As the mind is transformed to be more spacious, one can shift awareness to balance emotional ups and downs. The space allows the emotions to be felt but then released. Over time one becomes more experienced, leading to a sustained state of wellbeing, peace and joy.

There is a hum below the momentary experiences intertwined with the energy field that surrounds life. If the mind is transformed from the inside out to be soft, flexible and almost boundless, then one has the capacity to shift to a deeper level. The word "shift" is the key. An emotion erupts, for example one feels that one's heart is breaking, pain is vivid. Or one wakes up in the night overcome by worry. But then there can be redirection. It is just like in yoga when one pays attention to the arch in the left foot. But this time the attention moves to the big compassion in the heart below the affective dimension. I present imagery exercises throughout the book, so that practitioners can try them themselves to give an experiential base for leading the exercise with others. Try this imagery exercise to approximate this experience.

IMAGERY EXERCISE: THE HUM OF CREATION

Think about a particularly disturbing incident in the recent past. Where were you? What were you doing? Who was there? What were you feeling? Notice any perceptual details that come to mind: sights, sounds, kinesthetic movements, tactile touches or smells. Take yourself back to that moment vividly. Then find the place in your body where you have the strongest feeling. Where is it in the body? How big is it? What shape is it? Where does it lie: in the head, stomach or heart? How big is it? What color, what texture? This feeling is huge and you don't like it. You want whatever caused it out of your life. You feel desperate and that you can't stand it. Wait, wait, shift, shift, go to the big compassion in the heart under the feelings. Sense the compassionate heart that is connected to the hum of the universe. Feel the unending compassion and kindness that is the kernel of all creation. Take the attention into the chest and feel this beneath the heart. It seems like there is no end since it extends into space, and moves out to either side into the arms. As you focus on the compassion in your heart, the initial feeling softens and fades. You feel peaceful.

THE DOOR TO THE UNCONSCIOUS

All paths to wisdom lead to opening the door to the unconscious, creating a spacious mind. It is counterintuitive, because many think that controlling the mind and suppressing emotions is the way of transformation. But the paradoxical solution is surrendering and letting go of control to expand the inner world. Opening to the unconscious creates a sweet wind to blow away the clutter. Patanjali, the second century BCE compiler of the *Yoga Sutras* (Aranya 1963), compared the transformed mind to the sky. Emotions, sensations and thoughts occur like clouds in the sky, but they float through without overtaking awareness. This book shows the practitioner how to help others have a consistent experience of joy and peace. In other words, I give pointers on techniques to open the door to the unconscious for wisdom.

RELAXING THE EGO

The quest to transform the mind to wisdom is enhanced by relaxing the ego to contact the spiritual Self hiding in the unconscious. This can be done by focusing attention on something like a body sensation, the breath, a mantra or the visualization of an archetype. The firm barrier erected to the unconscious is loosened, and insight from the Self connected to the energy field finds a natural flow to consciousness. From a yoga perspective the *buddhi* or wisdom function has been developed (Rama *et al.* 1976). From a Buddhist perspective the mind has become empty and spacious. From a psychological perspective, the ego has become secure so that it can let go. When the mind becomes wise, experiential knowledge and spiritual wisdom can coexist in awareness.

People are naturally fascinated with archetypes such as the hero sports figure or the seductress pop star. Archetypes are hard to explain, but humans know one when they see it. An archetype is a recognizable collection of characteristics that capture human imagination. To understand an archetype it's best to explain the space where they originate. They reside in the energy domain, the invisible realm that underlies physical reality. This dimension may seem irrational to some, but even research in physics has established an energy field. Neutrinos, for example, have no mass, and millions pass through the earth and our bodies all the time. Psychologists, religious teachers and physicists use different words to describe this dimension beyond time and space. Carl Jung (1964) called it the collective unconscious, an invisible field that all humans are connected to which can be sensed through dreams and symbols. Buddhist philosophy (Ray 2001) teaches the concept of the Buddha mind that can be contacted when meditation practice empties the mind. Vedantic Hindu (Rama *et al.* 1976) tenants include the subtle plane accessible by transforming the mind through the various practices of yoga.

THE ENERGY FIELD

For the purposes of this book I am using the term "energy field." Elders of the Hopi tribe describe *katsinas* (Walters 1977), or spirits who come from the sacred mountains to bring gifts. According to these teachers, the katsinas are here next to us, invisible to the eye but active and felt by humans in their day-to-day lives. This is what the energy field is like, not a space above or below, but right here, underlying our daily reality. If people have the capability, they can expand perception beyond the material reality to the energy field. Both realities coexist together, but a transformation of consciousness is necessary to sense information from the energetic realm. This happens by opening the conscious mind to the unconscious. In turn, the mind is transformed to wisdom, to become spacious so that the dualities of the material and spiritual world can intertwine into awareness.

In both psychological and spiritual traditions, scholars propose an element in the human psyche connected to this energy field, the small, quiet voice within. I am using the term *atman*, translated from Sanskrit to mean spiritual Self. This designates the human faculty in the unconscious connected to the energy field. Humans are often cut off from this, since the ego in its natural quest for stability constricts consciousness. Natural psychological dynamics start working in infancy to establish a stable sense separate from the flow of consciousness. The ego acts to close the unconscious and to relegate more and more emotionally charged material there.

To become wise this process can be reversed. I am not saying that a person becomes like an infant again, awash in internal and external sensations. Childlike innocence may be a quality of a wise mind, but there is also an acute awareness. This awareness keeps a focus as the mind becomes more spacious.

Focusing on an archetype by visualizing it holds the unconscious open safely. This is important because the task of opening the mind can be fraught with difficulty. It can make one crazy to have memories and emotions pour into conscious awareness.

ARCHETYPAL IMAGERY

Imagining an archetype gives the mind stability, or something to hold onto as the deceptively concrete walls of the conscious mind become permeable. Over time as the mind becomes spacious, it isn't constricted to the stream of words moving in worrisome circles. Openness gives room for the rational mind to organize ideas and problem-solve. Rational reasoning can operate clearly and not be pushed aside by worries or depleted by the energy drain needed to keep the unconscious sealed. Also there is room for intuitive insights, and sensations and memories can be experienced vividly and released. Focusing on archetypes opens the window to the unconscious, letting the stale air out and allowing the inner world to breathe with life.

The idea that wisdom is the goal of human development arises from a holistic model. In this model humans are spiritual, mental, physical and emotional. The spiritual body is the localized energy field that surrounds the physical one, and the Self is hidden in each individual's unconscious. The information from the energy field is deep and profound, and sometimes transcends words. The language of the Self is intuition and images.

An open mind is a wise mind. This does not translate as a pinnacle of success, but rather a change in the inner world. The benefits of this transformation are great, including mental clarity, vitality, emotional balance, creativity, health and increased energy. Opening the mind creates spaciousness so thinking either rationally or intuitively can flow naturally, and, more importantly, images or sensations can flow from the Self connected to the energy field. As the mind becomes focused and relaxed, insights can pop up. Simultaneously, rational problem solving, experiential knowledge and sensations can operate unhindered. A spacious mind is accompanied by warmth, humor and softness as well.

There are a number of approaches to opening the unconscious. Psychology has many methods, and some are even polar opposites. One is to strengthen the ego so that it will relax; another is to imbue the ego with a rational voice, so emotions don't keep the conscious mind in a chaotic state. From spiritual traditions there are also varied practices, including meditation, observing rituals and following rules of conduct.

Using human fascination with archetypes as a point of focus can be a tool to open the unconscious. Choosing an archetype to identify with can help accomplish this. Archetypes have a singular effect on consciousness since they reside in the energy field, and are easily understood by the conscious mind since the unique collection of characteristics is personified. For example, the wise person archetype could be the Dalai Lama, Martin Luther King or Sister Teresa. Humans immediately recognize these icons as a representation of wisdom. Since an archetype not only resides in the energy field but is also personified in a human form, the ego is attracted to it. The ego disengages from its tendency to fortify the unconscious, and relaxes barriers. It is a natural and even an enjoyable exercise since archetypes are enticingly attractive to the human mind. The archetype becomes a window to open the unconscious, releasing material and transforming the mind to spaciousness. An encounter with an archetype can take many forms, but it is fueled by an attraction, like an itch that won't go away. If one is open, an archetype will present itself. Then one can consciously choose to continue with the encounter. Amplification or active imagination[3] can be used to expand the interaction. Finding images, stories or facts about it, making drawings and writing about it are all ways to explore the relationship and as a result open the unconscious.

---

3   These terms come from Carl Jung's writings as techniques for working
     with dreams.

As the book continues I will detail more dramatically how imagining archetypes can transform the mind to be wise for a sustained experience of peace and joy. Coaches and therapists will discover a powerful tool to help their clients develop a focus of attention in a fun, playful manner. Individual egos are naturally attracted to archetypes, and relax their hold on the barrier to the unconscious. Over time, suppressed emotions are released and a channel is opened to the spiritual Self in the unconscious. The mind becomes open and spacious. There is a fluid quality of what Hindu philosophers call the *chitta* or mind-stuff. Emotional strength results since sensations can be felt and released. Emotional stability, clarity of perception and spiritual insight create wisdom.

CHAPTER 1

OPENING THE UNCONSCIOUS

Sustained states of peace and joy don't just happen by thinking good thoughts, getting high with LSD, eating peyote, mapping a shamanic journey or meditating for a twelve-hour stretch. This transcendent consistency happens over time as people transform their inner world to spaciousness, thereby opening the unconscious. It took me a long time to learn these ideas during my graduate studies in psychology and my spiritual practices of yoga and Zen meditation.

Early in my spiritual path, in 1969, I heard Elmer Green (Green 1975) speak. He was a psychologist from the Menninger Foundation, studying mind–body potential. I was a graduate student at the University of Kansas located about 30 miles from Topeka, the site of the Foundation. The two brothers who founded it were followers of Freud and had made the center renowned for psychoanalytic studies. But in the 1970s it attracted psychologists working on the frontiers of the human potential movement. One of these was Elmer Green, whom I had recruited to come to KU for a Friday afternoon pro-seminar. I remember his talk in detail. Vivid memories can signify an important time in life when key decisions are made. I learned about this when I was working in a child development clinic in Oklahoma City. The head psychologist taught me about early recollections, citing the famous scholar Alfred Adler (2009). Key memories that accompany life's turning points are stored in a sensory-rich way. My vivid memory of Dr. Green's talk is that it marked the beginning of my lifelong quest. Since this lecture, I have been on a mission to help people open their unconscious minds to reach their potential, both spiritual and psychological.

Recalling his talk seems like playing a movie inside my head. I remember walking into the seminar room with steps descending in front of me. He was standing in the presenter's pit adjusting a transparency on an overhead machine, humming with a noisy fan. I looked at the projected symbol which was a circle like the one in Figure 1.1. The word "conscious" was at the top and the word "unconscious" was at the bottom. He said, "The unconscious becomes conscious, and the conscious becomes unconscious."

Figure 1.1 Green's view of the mind

The conscious becomes unconscious and the unconscious becomes conscious.
In his view yogis achieved this when they could control their heart
function and blood pressure. It is also a yogic view of enlightenment.

He pointed to the drawing, saying, "That's the purpose of yoga—to make the conscious unconscious and the unconscious conscious." This convoluted statement captured my attention and laid the foundation for my lifelong quest.

After showing the symbol, Green described his trip to India where he studied yogis who allegedly could stop their hearts. By hooking them up to EEG equipment and heart-rate monitors, he aimed to verify the physiological correlates of this phenomenon, and as a result to learn more about human potential. He explained, if he could discover how yogis stopped their hearts, then he could help humans expand the power of their minds. I was fascinated as Green turned on a video of a yogi sitting cross-legged on the floor in a hospital room. Several Indian doctors standing beside him were adjusting the electrodes on the yogi's temples and heart. The camera shifted to the equipment showing pins scoring waves across sheaths of paper.

Green commented that the yogi didn't actually stop his heart. Instead it went into extreme fibrillation which trapped blood as the heart muscle fluttered. There was no heartbeat, since blood wasn't moving. However, the yogi was calm and unmoving. I had seen another similar film of a North American man who could make his arm bleed at will. This man sat in a chair, and held his arm up clenching his fist. It was taut, and the man looked directly at his forearm. All of a sudden a small spot on the arm started bleeding. The man was asked, "How did you do this? How did you make your arm bleed?" The man answered, "I asked its permission to bleed."

Mind seemed to rule over matter. Conscious thought affected physiological function, the unconscious became conscious. This didn't make immediate sense to me. But as the lecture continued, I began to understand that the yogi and the bleeding man didn't achieve these marvels by concentrating on specific thoughts that would control their bodies. Instead they opened their minds in a passive manner, allowing subtle communication between conscious awareness and unconscious autonomic functions. Brain functions that occurred in the unconscious such as the beating of the heart, or the integrity of the skin, were influenced by a process that opened the mind.

Kobe Bryant, frequently the most valuable player in the NBA, is an example of a person whose mind is open to the unconscious. Often when a basketball player makes an unbelievable shot, the sportscaster says, "Wow, he was unconscious." After being blocked by several guards with walls of arms, Kobe fades, and miraculously finds an opening, sails over another guard while seemingly levitating five feet for a dunk shot. Obviously Kobe does not stop to create an executive plan for this shot. He surrenders control and lets his body and years of practice, fine-tuned muscle development and the gifts of eye–hand coordination take over as he becomes one with the ball and basket. This is an example of the conscious becoming unconscious for physical intelligence and skill. Green's drawing showed that this was what happens for all aspects of the being. The mind is relaxed, and the unconscious is open allowing enhanced potential.

Looking at models of the mind both from Western psychology and Eastern religious philosophy gives some guideposts for understanding what happens when the conscious mind opens to the unconscious.

FREUD'S MIND

Freud (1949) brought the concept of the unconscious mind into Western culture's awareness. He thought that humans were controlled by the unconscious. For him the id or the need for sex and survival resided there and was the most formidable force in explaining aberrations in human behavior. My favorite example of this phenomenon is President Bill Clinton's sexual liaison with Monica Lewinsky which resulted in his impeachment. People ask, "Why would a smart and powerful man risk his career with such an unethical and stupid mistake?" The answer is clear: there were unconscious forces afoot compelling Clinton's behavior.

Sigmund Freud suggested that the mind had a finite amount of psyche energy, and the unconscious was like a hydraulic system. Mental energy was needed to keep things sealed up outside of conscious awareness. Traumatic events that are too intense for a person to integrate are shoved into the unconscious, and as a result less and less mind power is available for day-to-day activities. Freud's dream analysis was designed to release material from the unconscious so that a human had more available mind energy. He didn't necessarily want to open the unconscious like Green mentions as the yogi's goal, but he didn't want memories trapped there to restrict the stream of consciousness (see Figure 1.2).

Emotional health was the goal of Freud's viewpoint. If a human is emotionally healthy, then mental energy would not keep traumatic memories and emotions trapped in the unconscious. Instead the human mind would be fluid to choose actions, as opposed to being emotionally reactive as things erupted from the unconscious outside of conscious control. Possibly Hillary Clinton is a model of a person with a mind that has released suppressed trauma. Instead of being full of rage and vengeful about Bill's outrageous infidelity, she handled it with grace. People whose unconscious minds are sealed with a trap-door are quite reactive. Something happens that is insulting or degrading to them, and there is anger, revenge or petty acts of spite. It could have been that Hillary called Monica Lewinsky to leave hate messages, or stole the stained blue dress and burned it. But it does not appear she did. Instead, her inner world was such that she could be reflective in her actions and think what was best for her, her career and her family. It is an interesting concept that one becomes strong psychologically when suppressed unconscious material is released.

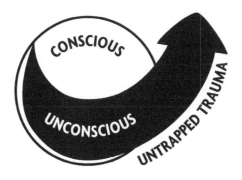

Figure 1.2 Freud's conception of the mind

Dream analysis was used to release information buried in the unconscious which keeps a person from emotional health. This keeps the unconscious from controlling day-to-day activities without the individual's awareness. Dream analysis was a precursor of using images or thinking in pictures to open the unconscious.

THE TAO OR THE WAY

Carl Jung (1970) was one of Freud's colleagues who shared some basic concepts. While Freud worked with neurotics (people who are overcome with anxiety), Jung worked in a hospital for schizophrenics (people whose reality is delusion). He noticed that there was consistency in the images from his patients' dreams. Even though they were crazy, their fractured minds seemingly picked up ideas from a shared, invisible dimension. Jung studied with a Chinese scholar integrating the concept of the Tao (Lao

Tzu and Legge 2012), often translated as "the way" and signifying the creative force that underlies material reality. Jung thought that dreams must pick up some information from the Tao as he proposed the collective unconscious.

A person who exemplifies living the Tao would show a natural equilibrium, with flexibility to flow back and forth between opposites. When I think about this, one of my friends comes to mind. His name is Joe. He is not famous and may even appear shy in groups. The main quality he projects, though, is balance, not acting out of just one or the other side of the Tao. The yin side is expansive, and the yang side is dense. Being overly yin, a person would be highly emotional and overwhelmed, whereas having too much yang would indicate a person might be depressed and aggressive. Joe seems to hang out in the middle of the Tao. There is a stillness or quietness in his nature. He observes clearly and seems to understand the big picture and the correct way of proceeding, showing a conscious awareness. Opening the unconscious for a natural flow from the energetic domain to the conscious mind is being balanced in the Tao. (See Figure I.2 in the Introduction for a depiction of the Tao, or the invisible force underlying creation, which influenced Jung's idea of the collective unconscious.)

JUNG'S MIND

Jung used the concept of the invisible energy field, the Tao, and called it the collective unconscious. He said that the visions that the schizophrenics experienced came from here. He divided the mind as Freud did. But unlike Freud, where only the id resided in the unconscious, to Jung the unconscious was also connected to the collective. In his theory, archetypes or identifiable energy patterns resided there. He had three basic archetypes: the shadow, or things that human suppress or that they don't know about themselves; the anima, or female; and the animus or male. According to Jung, humans identify with an archetype at different times as a way of expressing parts of the self which are hidden in the unconscious. For example, Clinton was acting out his shadow with Monica Lewinsky.

A human can consciously choose to move material out of the unconscious so that they are not controlled by it. Over time, identification with an archetype can open the unconscious material, creating a spacious and ultimately wise mind. Jung recommended opening the unconscious with dream interpretation, as did Freud, but the goal was to bring the whole mind into awareness, which he called the Self. When this happens there is a natural flow from the collective unconscious which not only aids emotional health by releasing material in the shadow, but also allows for spiritual insight. With Jung, the spiritual and psychological commingle. Jung said that a person could not be ethical unless the shadow was opened since the unconscious could prompt actions outside of conscious awareness.

The main quality of a person who has opened the unconscious would be a refined awareness, and a palatable quality of amiability. I have a colleague named Peter who personifies this. Peter has a quiet, yet strong demeanor. At faculty meetings, people would listen when he talked, since he didn't speak frivolously. When I sat beside him, I wanted to put my head on his shoulder. He emanated spirituality without speaking of it. He was calm and thoughtful, but at the same time could passionately express an opinion. Things hidden in the unconscious did not get in the way of his actions or interactions.

Jung thought that the goal of human development was spiritual as well as emotional. His view was that one needed to open the shadow which contained the basic archetypes of the anima (the feminine) and the animus (the masculine) to bring awareness to the whole of the mind which was the Self. He borrowed the Self from Vedantic Hindu philosophy where the Self, or *atman*, is the spiritual focus of the individual. When one opens the unconscious, one would not be controlled by those influences; instead there is an open conduit to the collective unconscious (see Figure 1.3).

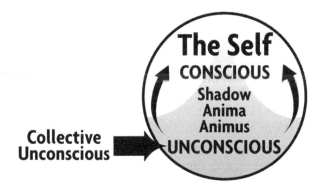

Figure 1.3 Image depicting Jung's view of the basic archetypes, the anima, the animus and the shadow, in relation to the collective unconscious

THE HINDU MIND

There are also models from Eastern religious philosophy which shed light on creating a wise mind. Vedantic Hinduism (Rama 1976), based on the ancient books, the Rig Vedas, written around 1000 BC, taught that the goal of spiritual practice was to transform the mind to enlightenment. This happened through the eight limbs of yoga which begin with attitudes and asana (postures) and end with Samadhi or enlightenment. In this philosophy, the mind is flooded with sensations and is overcome with memories that erupt automatically. The eight limbs of practice teach humans to focus the mind so that the *buddhi*, or wisdom, develops. Concentrating attention lets the memory banks empty and allows emotions and sensations to pass through unheeded. This is reminiscent of Freud's opening suppressed emotions, and Jung's release of the shadow. Their models prescribed dream interpretation or identification with archetypes so that mental obstructions can move up and out of the unconscious, but in the Vedantic system, spiritual practice develops the *buddhi*. This focus creates space which allows clutter from the mind to be released.

With the development of the *buddhi*, awareness can join with the spiritual Self, called the *atman*, since this part of the mind is connected to the energy field (see Figure 1.4). A channel is opened so that spiritual insight can pop into conscious awareness.

Nelson Mandela might be an example of someone whose mind has transformed in this way. He had a focus of attention in his goal of liberating South Africa. His *buddhi* was well developed so that he was open to the *atman* to infuse his life with spiritual purpose.

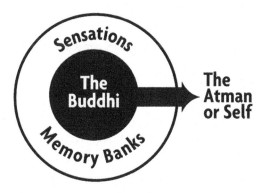

Figure 1.4 This is a simplified graphic of the Vedantic mind without the Sanskrit words, except for buddhi *and* atman

But it shows the essence, that the path of wisdom is to develop the *buddhi* (wisdom function) through meditation or yoga, which allows one to keep a focus through the perceptual sensations and the erupted flow of memories. Once the *buddhi* is developed one can transform the mind to sense the *atman* or the spiritual Self.

In the Buddhist view, the mind is to be emptied to join with the Buddha mind (Loori 2008), which, like the Tao, is the invisible, creative force that underlies the material world. Practice in meditation releases internal thoughts, memories and events. In this way there is no inhibition between awareness and the Buddha mind.

THE WISE MIND

To create a model for changing the mind to be wise I've taken concepts from each of these views including the ideas of Green, Freud and Jung, as well as Taoist and Hindu philosophies (Nelson 2007). The whole mind is both emotionally healthy and spiritually aware. The mechanics of accomplishing this go something like the following:

- A focus of attention relaxes the mind.

- The unconscious opens.

- Emotional material is released.

- The mind becomes spacious, allowing three things:

    ○ emotions are sensed and released

    ○ unconscious motivation is diffused

    ○ spiritual insight is freed.

Jung had his basic three archetypes, the shadow, anima and animus. But I take archetypes more metaphorically. To me it is a personification, symbol or object that creates a pattern of recognizable characteristics. The human mind is fascinated with archetypes. For example, think of the popularity of sports figures that embody the idea of a hero, or a movie star who exudes the essence of a seductress. There are many, many archetypes and a human can find an archetype to his or her liking, focus on it, and identify with it. This acts to open the unconscious using a natural psychological dynamic of human attraction with archetypes. Imagining an archetype functions as a window to the unconscious, allowing trapped memories and emotions to be released, simultaneously fine-tuning focusing skills as the mind imagines the archetype. Over time, the mind empties, becomes more spacious and fluid with the energy field, naturally connecting with the world of spirit. Visualizing archetypes relaxes the ego and opens the unconscious in a safe manner, preventing distress at the release of material. The focus on the archetype over time creates the ability to hold attention as insights come from the energy field.

The key in Figure 1.5 is the archetype. Focusing on an archetype by visualizing it holds the unconscious open safely. This is important because the task of opening the mind can be fraught with difficulty. It can make one crazy to have memories and emotions pour into conscious awareness. A psychologist named Stanislav Grof (1989) called such an experience a "spiritual emergency." During the heyday of the human potential movement from the 1970s and even up through the 1990s, some so-called spiritual teachers helped people create such chaotic mental states by having them hyperventilate. I had students at Prescott College who joined a group we all termed "the breathers." People became obsessed with frenzied states. However, a gentler approach is to capitalize on the natural psychodynamics of archetypal fascination.

*Figure 1.5 The archetype in this model acts as a window
between the conscious and the unconscious*

ARCHETYPAL IMAGERY STAGES

Imagining an archetype gives the mind stability, or something to hold onto as the deceptively concrete walls of the conscious mind become permeable. Over time as the mind becomes spacious, it isn't constricted to the stream of words moving in worrisome circles. Openness gives room for the rational mind to organize ideas and problem-solve. Rational reasoning can operate clearly and not be pushed aside by worries or depleted by the energy drain needed to keep the unconscious sealed (see Figure 1.6).

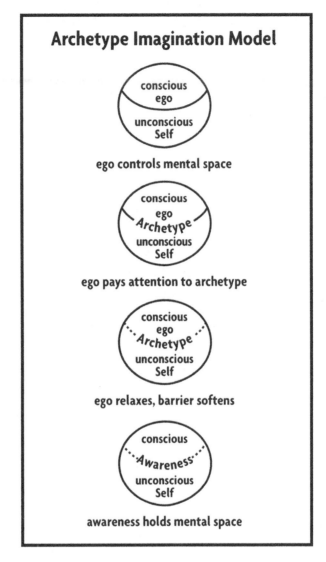

Figure 1.6 Archetypal imagery stages

These are the stages of transforming consciousness when using archetypal imagery to create a more spacious mind.

THE WISE MIND–BODY MODEL

To create a diagram to show how the mind can be transformed to wisdom, I propose four bodies of the human being. These are spiritual, physical, emotional and mental. The physical is closely aligned to the Self as it responds to intuition, as in a gut feeling. Many spiritual practices focus on the body. Examples are practicing yoga or in following the breath in meditation. Therefore bringing awareness into the physical body assists in the transformation of the mind to wisdom.

The emotional body rests inside the physical body and is highly reactive, influenced by memories and sensations. But it does have a natural connection to the spiritual body through primitive intuition. If the mind becomes spacious and simultaneously has a focus, it can sense the emotions and the intuition they carry, as opposed to being overwhelmed by sensations.

The mental body is inside of the emotional one. Most people think they are the thoughts that are rolling through their mind, but this is because the ego is restricting awareness from other parts of the mind in an effort to create stability. It does this by moving memories to the unconscious. Awareness, or conscious thought for most people, is tied to the ego, and contact to the Self is limited to bursts of insight that might make their way through the closed mental body. To become wise the ego can be relaxed so information from the other bodies can pop into awareness. The mental body has now transcended the ego to become a holder of awareness. Infants create a stable sense of self by having the ego close off the stream of consciousness from the spiritual body. This is important. But over time, the ego shuts down connections with the other bodies due to difficult life events. The path to wisdom is to relax the ego, so that insight can spring from the other bodies to consciousness. The emotional body expresses primitive intuition but can easily take over consciousness with strong sensations. However, relaxing the ego allows emotions to be sensed and then released. The physical body has a direct connection to the spiritual body since it is not inhibited by the ego. That is why meditation and yoga use physical movements and focus on the breath. Imagery and focusing on archetypes does this too.

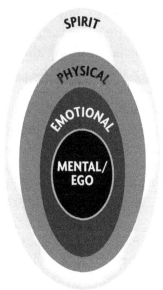

The Four Bodies

Figure 1.7 The four bodies of the being are mental, emotional, physical and spiritual

The quest to transform the mind to wisdom is enhanced by relaxing the ego. This can be done by focusing attention on something that the ego likes by focusing on a body sensation in yoga, the breath, a mantra or the visualization of an archetype. The firm barrier erected to the unconscious is loosened, and insight from the Self connected to the energy field finds a natural flow to consciousness. From a Buddhist perspective the mind has become empty, and this spaciousness allows spiritual awareness. From a psychological perspective, the ego has become secure enough to let go. When the mind becomes wise, experiential knowledge and spiritual wisdom can coexist in awareness. Developing a focus of attention by meditation, prayer or imagining archetypes relaxes the ego, allowing buried material in the unconscious to release. The ego is also fascinated by archetypes since they personify human characteristics. The dotted lines in Figure 1.8 show that consciousness has become more permeable. Instead of the ego controlling the mind, a focus of awareness holds the mind. In this fluid state, consciousness becomes more spacious and allows the mind to perceive insight from all four bodies.

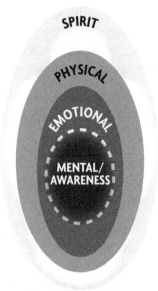

The Wise Mind-Body

Figure 1.8 The Wise Mind–Body model
The ego likes to pay attention to things, and focusing on
images or pictures naturally opens the unconscious.

WISDOM CHARACTERISTICS

As a person's mind becomes more whole and moves to approximate
wisdom there may be internal qualities that reflect this change.
There is no test that determines a wise mind, but a person can
notice things inside and out indicating transformation. Sharing
wisdom characteristics with clients may help them map inner
changes and give clues to validate their process to work towards
health and awareness. Some of the characteristics look like the
following:

- *Synchronicity.* If happy coincidences occur, it is a good
  sign. One walks to the right place at the right time. For
  example, an accidental turn can result in running into an
  acquaintance not seen for several years. Or by chance one
  is looking for a phone number and happens to open the
  phone book to the right place, with the number staring
  one in the face. This type of serendipity is a gentle nudge

that one is opening to the spiritual Self inside, leading to timely intersections. This idea is similar to the story of a Buddhist monk, who leans down to smell a flower and inadvertently misses a blow from an enemy's sword.

- *Kindness.* Feeling compassion inside and showing that to others is an natural, automatic extension of the inner transformation.

- *Heightened intuition.* One might find that one starts doing healthy things automatically, changing one's diet or going on early morning walks.

- *Increased awareness of one's own behavior.* Interactional patterns that one never noticed before become vividly clear. For example if one usually fights with a family member and thinks that it is her fault. All of a sudden one sees one's own behavior that might prompt the attack. One's participation in the negative interaction becomes clear instead of blaming others.

- *Feeling love.* Feeling connected to spiritual forces, and feeling that unending compassion inside and out, is an excellent pat on the back that the transformation inside has happened.

These external signs can show a person that he or she is transforming the mind to wisdom.

For the remainder of this book, I will present how archetypal imagery can help coaches and therapists help their clients. The practitioner may want to experiment with the imagery while reading the book. Adopting a playful approach is a great way to use one's intuition. This playful practice will lay the experiential foundation to help others imagine archetypes. Think about finding ways to look at historical figures, mythic heroes and heroines, deities or objects of art. Pop into a museum and look at statues and see which one awakens a keen body attraction. Browse the art section of a bookstore and a pick up a book that strikes your fancy. Flip through pictures until you connect with one. Once you find one, surf the Internet and find a picture or story. Spend a few minutes visualizing the figure. Later chapters offer quizzes for your clients to begin an encounter with an archetype in a more determined way. But this lighthearted beginning will set the stage.

What would people be like if they had changed their inner world to have a wise mind? First, their energy would be magnetic. One would want to sit next to a wise person. One could sit nearby and not talk, or alternatively have a conversation that would be comfortable. This person would seem present here and now, and not be preoccupied, jittery or tense. Both playful and reflective, the person could come up with surprises. Anger could be there but it could evaporate as soon as it came. Most importantly, the person would be embodying wisdom.

CHAPTER 2

WISDOM AND THE OPEN MIND

The following story shows that humans sometimes have a limited perception of the true nature of reality. It is an Indian legend of six blind men touching an elephant and then trying to explain what this creature was like:

> It was six men of Indostan
> To learning much inclined,
> Who went to see the Elephant
> (Though all of them were blind),
> That each by observation
> Might satisfy his mind.
>
> The First approached the Elephant,
> And happening to fall
> Against his broad and sturdy side,
> At once began to bawl:
> "God bless me! but the Elephant
> Is very like a wall!"
>
> The Second, feeling of the tusk
> Cried, "Ho! what have we here,
> So very round and smooth and sharp?
> To me 'tis mighty clear
> This wonder of an Elephant
> Is very like a spear!"

The Third approached the animal,
And happening to take
The squirming trunk within his hands,
Thus boldly up he spake:
"I see," quoth he, "the Elephant
Is very like a snake!"

The Fourth reached out an eager hand,
And felt about the knee:
"What most this wondrous beast is like
Is mighty plain," quoth he;
"'Tis clear enough the Elephant
Is very like a tree!"

The Fifth, who chanced to touch the ear,
Said: "E'en the blindest man
Can tell what this resembles most;
Deny the fact who can,
This marvel of an Elephant
Is very like a fan!"

The Sixth no sooner had begun
About the beast to grope,
Than, seizing on the swinging tail
That fell within his scope.
"I see," quoth he, "the Elephant
Is very like a rope!"

And so these men of Indostan
Disputed loud and long,
Each in his own opinion
Exceeding stiff and strong,
Though each was partly in the right,
And all were in the wrong!

Indian legend retold by John Godfrey Saxe (1963)

Wisdom is the ability to perceive the whole of the elephant, not just being fooled into thinking a part defines the whole. Some scholars have used the word transconceptual (Walsh 2011) to describe this phenomenon. Reality is perceived from a bigger arena than from the viewpoint of a human's enmeshed ego creating a narrow field of perception. An inner transformation can be accompanied by clarity of perception to integrate knowledge, experience and intuitive spiritual insight. This chapter reviews different perspectives and definitions of wisdom that will help coaches and therapists to convey this concept to their clients, as a tool to motivate the use of archetypal imagery as a powerful transformation tool.

WISE PEOPLE

Wise people have a warmth and equanimity that philosophers have tried to describe. Thirteenth century philosopher Thomas Aquinas (Aquinas 1923; Bergsma and Ardelt 2012) said that of all human pursuits, wisdom was the most sublime and delightful. He coined the word "life-ability" for wisdom, conveying that it is a holistic phenomenon. It combines knowledge and experience resulting in the ineffable ability to make one's life work by perceiving at a deep level the nature of the reality that one inhabits. A person who embodies wisdom conveys a continual cheerfulness. As mentioned earlier, Chögyam Trungpa (1991), Tibetan Rinpoche, said that a wise mind is warm, friendly, humorous and spacious.

All of these ideas convey that wise people are different than others, and part of this difference is their demeanor which results from a certain inner change. Their transformation commingles cognitive, emotional and spiritual dimensions.

WISE PEOPLE AND EGO TRANSCENDENCE

Wise people have a realm of self beyond everyday ego. This emotional maturity is sometimes called ego integration, integrity or transcendence. Western psychologists document the stages that lead to this transformation.

Robert Kegan (1998), a developmental psychologist at Harvard, created a theory of cognitive development. He proposes a number of stages, beginning with "the impulsive mind" as children aged two through six react impulsively to the world around them. As people age they move through five stages, ending with what he terms "a self-transforming mind." He also calls this the interindividual stage (Kegan 1982). In this stage a person develops ego transcendence. The inner world changes to allow the human perception of interdependence, transcending a subjective individual perspective.

Erik Erikson (1994) was a developmental psychologist who created a framework for understanding psychosocial growth throughout the life span. According to him, wisdom is not just expert knowledge, but also includes actual changes in consciousness. He formulated eight stages, and in each one humans have a maturation task to move towards health and maturity. For example "competence" was the stage for children aged 6–12, and the task was to move from inferiority to industry. His last stage included the task to move towards ego integrity instead of despair. Ego integrity implies an expansion from a limited view of the self and others. This leads to more mental space since mental activity is freed from fears and anxiety of a limited perception of the self. The goal of therapy or coaching is to help someone gain a clearer awareness of the self, which can allow insights and healing to take place, eventually moving a person to wisdom.

Both Kegan and Erikson specify that emotional maturity, that is, ego integrity or a self-transforming mind, happens with age. However, if tools exist to prompt ego integration at earlier points in development, the mind could become wise at any point in development. The main issue is creating openness to reality so that it is perceived in a more fundamental way.

Other Western psychologists link openness to wisdom. For example, Lancaster and Palframan (2009) say wisdom requires a person to have openness to perceive the self beyond the everyday ego. When this happens, there is a continual movement of awareness into the unconscious to sense the totality of self moving people to a spiritual dimension. Paradoxically, a psychological process, ego integration, opens the mind to the spiritual dimension.

PRAJNAPARAMITA, THE PERFECTION OF WISDOM
There is an archetype that is actually named wisdom in the Buddhist traditions of Vajrayana (Tibetan) and Zen. Her name is

Prajnaparamita, and the name translated from Sanskrit means the perfection of wisdom. Prajna is wisdom, and paramita is literally to go beyond or to go to the other shore (Loori 2008). This means that wisdom is not just thinking better and having more knowledge and using logic more skillfully. It is actually thinking in a *different* way. The difference is that a space is created that allows clarity of perception apart from ego identification and also gives room for the interplay of mind functions, rational, intuitive, body sensations and memory. This space also allows spiritual awareness.

Joanna Macy (1991), a Buddhist and sustainable systems scholar, says that Paramita is the mother of all Buddhas. When people sense her energy the illusion of ego is lost. Macy uses a thought-provoking phrase to describe Paramita: the pregnant zero. Zero is a great metaphor for wise thinking. All is the same in zero, symbolically holding nothing and at the same time being all-inclusive, holding everything. Zero is a circle with no ending or beginning, empty of preconception.

In early scriptures about Paramita, wisdom was described as teaching moral conduct, similar to philosophers who define wisdom as following normative ethics. But following rules, even though important, is not necessarily a mark of wisdom, because it does not require thinking in a different way. This was conveyed in later writings about Paramita. Wisdom wasn't simply following rules, but was the ability to change the mind so that it could perceive the interdependence of reality. The mind is freed and is open to light and space. Robert Walsh (2011), transpersonal psychologist, calls this a transconceptual way of knowing, seeing into the nature of self and reality.

WISDOM AND PARADOX

While some have written how the archetype Prajnaparamita shows that wisdom is the ability to open the mind to a spaciousness that is beyond dualities, others write about wisdom as paradox. Csikszentmihalyi and Nakamura (2005), popular business writers, stressed the paradoxical nature of wisdom since it not only includes rational and experiential knowledge but also the sacred or divine. Since wisdom is holistic it is both rational and non-rational. Non-rational is not the same as irrational. For example, it is irrational to say that the Earth is the center of the universe, since we know through the logic of science that the Earth rotates around the Sun, and its galaxy, the Milky Way. But for centuries indigenous people knew their relation to the Sun and envisioned this as a circle, building stone observatories from Stonehenge in the British Isles to medicine wheels in Montana. They sensed that the Earth's cycles represented in circles mirrored the earth's relationship to the Sun. This knowledge was non-rational, in that it didn't come to them through logic, but was rather a combination of the intuitive sense heightened by ceremonies and the experiential knowledge of observations.

Cognitive paradox is also described as non-dualistic thinking. This is the flexibility of not thinking that only one way is the right one and the rest wrong, allowing opposites to coexist in the mind. To put it in psychological terms, the benefits to the individual could exist alongside the benefits to others. Macy, in her description of Paramita, describes her as non-dualistic in that she represents interconnection of life. She is the personification of the principle of dependent co-arising, which means that all are connected in the energy field, and a shift in one element will have an effect on other elements.

The open mind can be non-dualistic since it doesn't jump from one polar opposite to another, but has space to consider both. As in the Heisenberg uncertainty principle in which energy can be measured either by a location or a movement, paradoxical thinking is "going beyond" rational knowing by creating a spacious mindscape where opposites and many possibilities can exist.

SOPHIA'S WISDOM

Over the years other archetypes have appeared to me. I stumbled on Sophia when I made up my nurses' story that I present in the Introduction. She popped into my mind in a surprising manner. Spiritual masters such as Paramahansa Yogananda (2005), author of *Autobiography of a Yogi*, teach that all great spiritual ideas come through intuition. Because of this, I thought it was auspicious that she had come to me from insight. The story I told at the psychoneuroimmunology workshop in Phoenix became very popular. People asked for it again and again.

Because of the story's surprising notoriety, I decided to do a little research about Sophia. Just as my intuition had supplied her name, it helped me find books and many references about her. I could walk into a store, and go directly to a book that contained her name. It seemed that she was all around me. For example, I found the book, *Sophie's World: A Novel About the History of Philosophy*, by Jostein Gaarder and Paulette Moller (2007). They point out that "sophy" in the word philosophy is an iteration of her name. This archetype had been hiding from me in plain sight. According to Susan Cady (Cady *et al.* 1986), a feminist theologian, Sophia is a red thread hiding throughout history.

The word Sophia is a derivation of the Greek word for wisdom and the Greek word *sophos* meaning "to be of the same kind" (Cady *et al.* 1986). This definition is exemplified in the Gnostic story in which Sophia is named as the spiritual creator. In this account the material universe emerges out of her own being, different than the traditional view of a father looking down and creating the universe separate from himself. In the Gnostic story, Sophia's own energy divides and subdivides exponentially to create all planets, stars, rocks, trees, fish and mammals. All creation is of "the same kind" as the creator. Her archetype taught me that I had a piece of her inside of me, and I needed to find it.

Vladimir Soloviev (1978), a Russian Orthodox priest, created a theology featuring Sophia. He called it "sophiology." As a boy he would look at the mountains of his native Russia and be filled with awe at the experience of "God in nature." His experiences countered the traditional Christian teaching that the natural world was base after the fall from grace of Adam and Eve. Soloviev found his experiences undeniable, countering this teaching. He still believed that he could find God in nature, even though it was an unorthodox view.

I traveled to Istanbul, Turkey, to see the cathedral named after Sophia built by the Byzantium emperor, Constantine II, one of the first rulers to convert to Christianity. The Hagia Sophia was erected on the same physical site as a temple to the Greek goddess

Artemis, later to become the Roman goddess Diana (Freely 1998). Both goddesses represented nature. Artemis brought spring each year, and Diana was the huntress who communed with animals. It is surprisingly unlike other European cathedrals. First, the floor was painted as if it were the surface of the earth, and the great domed ceiling was depicted as the sky. Second, the cathedral was built in a form more like a circle than a cross, since its elements were of equal length. The Hagia rests on the remnants of a nature goddess temple, the structure depicts the earth as its base, and its form approximates a circle, a symbol of the planet depicting the earth as spiritual. The route to the spiritual was through nature not above it. The path to transcendence was transforming one's inner world to find the spirit hidden there.

To some psychologists Sophia is a very important archetype. Jungian Marie-Louise von Franz (1985) writes about Sophia, claiming that she is the blueprint of all life on Earth or the *archetypal mundus*, meaning the very first archetype.

There is a Middle Eastern story about Sophia, the angel or aeon. She was the brightest of all the angels, but she had this bad habit of asking God questions, particularly about humans since she was keenly interested, watching them on the Earth from the heavens. For the offense of being too uppity with her questions, she was thrown out of heaven, and fell to Earth becoming clothed in skin and taking human form. She landed near the Red Sea. With no idea of how to make a living, she became a prostitute birthing many children. Through her sojourn, Sophia began to understand people and the choices that humans face in their lives. God looked down and was pleased at her humility, thereby reinstating her in heaven. However, she was no longer the brightest angel, but the lowliest. This shows that becoming wise isn't overcoming one's human nature, but moving inside and essentially becoming oneself.

SOPHIA AND THE WISDOM PATH

Sophia as an archetype depicts the path to wisdom. She shows the spiritual side of being wise. As the Gnostic creator her energy subdivided so a spiritual piece was in each atom of creation.

Metaphorically, each human has a piece of Sophia inside of them. Opening the mind to the unconscious allows a person to contact and listen to that creative spark.

Wise people have:

- the qualities of equanimity and cheerfulness

- emotional maturity, because they have detached from a limited perception of the self and have ego integration

- an open mind that allows the interplay of emotions, intuition, rational thought

- the ability to think paradoxically

- a keen sense of the interdependence of life

- embodiment of spirituality.

Wisdom is the ability to think *differently*, in such a way that one positions the self within the array of life on the Earth. There is no longer a self-absorbed view of the world, awash in emotions, fears and anxieties. There is an emotional strength that is noticeable. The mind is changed to become spacious and open, and increases in capability by its ability to think paradoxically. A wise person has a perspective that is permeable to creativity and typified by an awareness that holds a space for integration. Some philosophers use the metaphor that a wise person can sense the regions of the moon, always clear and serene. Wise people can inhabit a vast array of space for the mind to wander since sense of self is liberated from the individual ego.

WISDOM AS A GOAL OF COACHING OR THERAPY

This chapter reviewed psychologists' and philosophers' views on wisdom, and presented two archetypes of wisdom, Prajnaparamita and Sophia. It is clear that wisdom is a holistic phenomenon that includes expert knowledge, experience and a sacred dimension. As a path it is paradoxical because it requires psychological changes to release spiritual awareness. This is called ego integration or ego transcendence. Coaches and therapists can use this information to motivate clients in creating ego integration on the spiritual path. In this way clients can see the spiritual and emotional path as one. Creating space in the mind happens by ego integration. This in turn allows the unconscious to open, widening the view and even perception of the self and reality. It allows inspiration in waking consciousness.

CHAPTER 3

THE TRICKY EGO AND THE OPEN MIND

Humans want the experience of peace and joy, but this is tricky and elusive. In the last chapter, I talked about opening the unconscious to create a wise mind. This would be easy if a human could just say, "Okay, now, I'm opening the unconscious." But it doesn't work that way. Just like the drug problem in the United States couldn't be solved by Nancy Reagan's advice of just saying no, there are natural psychological dynamics that prevent consciousness from opening up, primarily the ego and emotions. These two are related. The ego gives the mind stability and defends from supposed attack to identity and security. When events appear unsafe to the individual, emotions erupt, allowing the ego to defend its territory. Understanding how emotions and the ego operate can motivate people to begin to make some changes to put these forces in their rightful place and open to wisdom. In this chapter I share some hard-fought lessons I've learned from errors on the path. Hopefully this will help the reader avoid them.

A VISIT TO THE DALAI LAMA

Early on in my journey, I thought I would become emotionless. When I was teaching in India, I was excited to visit the Dalai Lama whom I considered a model of spirituality. I thought, no doubt he can control all of his emotions. Most people think that the Dalai Lama radiates spirituality with sustained peace and joy. But I had a few surprises when I visited his residence in McLeod

Gang, a tiny town, up the mountain from Dharamsala in the northern Indian state of Himachal Pradesh. My family and I were there when I was teaching in India. As we drove up the valley we caught a spectacular glimpse of one of the tallest mountains on the Earth. The next day we trekked out of the community and within a few steps saw stone huts growing out of the ground with honey-colored grain drying on their roofs. In the mornings, we heard monks chanting with the exotic tones of humming more than one note simultaneously. Needless to say, it was an awe-inspiring location. One day as my daughter and I were walking around town, we saw a sign, "Foreigners: If you want to see the Dalai Lama, register your passport and come to the temple grounds at 1:00 pm today."

Of course, we wanted to do this. So after finding the right office to register our passports we joined the long lines outside his official residence. It was an amazing site. Near us, in the courtyard, we saw pairs of young monks in maroon and saffron robes eagerly slapping their hands as they made points in a debate. The Dalai Lama is not only the religious head of the Kagyupa or red hat Tibetan Buddhist sect (Tenzin Gyatso 1982), but at that time he also was the head of state of the exiled government of Tibet. Therefore extra security measures were required. To be searched, women went in one line and men in another. My daughter and I filed into a small house on the women's side, to be patted down by Tibetans wearing indigo brocaded robes, bright red sashes and polished chunks of turquoise around their necks. Leaving this house, as we queued up to go into the garden, we saw six or seven Tibetan monks standing in a line. Across from them was a Tibetan gardener doing prostrations, his hoe lying beside him. All the signs were present that we were going to meet a spiritual person.

As we got nearer, one monk handed each of us a red string before we stood in front of him. The Dalai Lama's presence was powerful, quiet, clear and strong, and he had no expression on his face except a quiet contentment. I thought, "This is what it is like to be spiritual all the time." But I had a surprise later in the week when I went to see a documentary film that showed him in a very different light.

One night, walking around McLeod Gang, we happened on a movie being shown in the courtyard of an elementary school. We walked through the gate and took a seat. Soon an old 16 millimeter machine projected a film about the search for the incarnation of a Rinpoche who had died several years before. In the film, the Dalai Lama directs his lamas to go into Tibet and elude Chinese authorities to visit a boy who had shown signs predicted by an oracle. He instructed them to show the boy various objects which had belonged to the former Rinpoche to see if he could pick them. As the lamas received instructions for the trip, they were bent over, prostrating themselves before their guru. It seemed as if they were cowering as he gave them directions in an angry voice. To me, this seemed like a totally different individual from the calmed, controlled persona during the reception for foreign visitors. But I knew the Dalai Lama was still in a state of sustained spirituality even though he was yelling.

My first major learning about creating a wise mind was that it is not about having only "good" emotions. Usually we think that being calm is good, whereas being angry or sad is bad, and the state to pursue is to be controlled and emotionless. But obviously this was wrong, as I saw the Dalai Lama take on different emotions. A mind that has been transformed still has strong emotions, but they do not stay. The wise mind has space, almost as a room with all the windows open. The wind can blow through. Emotions occur and then move out, just like wind blowing through the windows of a room.

DESIRES AND AFFIRMATIONS

Another mistaken notion I had was that if bad things happened to me, then I wasn't on the right path. Whenever I was sick, my New Age friend would say to me, "Why have you drawn this to yourself?" This made me feel I had done something wrong and that I wasn't being spiritual enough. If I acted correctly, then good things would be happening to me and I would be healthy. Not only that, but I would also have my desires met in terms of job, relationships, house and income. Of course, I had a sense that this might not be the case. I remember seeing a movie by Alan Watts (1999), a Zen teacher in the 1960s, which featured a Zen monk who had lost a leg to cancer and was in the process of dying. He beamed beatifically as he talked about Zen teachings, and the narrator asked if he was angry at his cancer. He started laughing, and as the movie ended Watts laughed as well, saying this was the best form of meditation. Obviously, the monk did not think that spirituality was the same as not being sick or getting what he wanted. It made him laugh to think that he should be upset about a fatal illness.

Prosperity consciousness is popular in the New Age press. For example, the book *The Secret* (Byrne 2006) tells how to create material wealth, be it a house, money, lover or whatever the heart desires. Another item from the popular press, Shakti Gawain's *Creative Visualization* (2002), first published in the 1980s, had the same message. Back in those days, I had a lot of friends writing affirmations of what they wanted to happen. It didn't seem quite right to me to try to get what you want and be spiritual at the same time. I thought the New Age phrase of "dying to the ego" was more consistent with ancient teachings.

Some traditions do link spiritual development with material wealth. A case in point is the ancient Chinese philosophy, Taoism, which teaches that if a person lives in balance with nature then prosperity will come. Feng shui, the practice of arranging the home for material wealth, is an offshoot of Taoism. The Calvinist who settled North America thought that having riches was a mark of being godly. Similarly, in Hinduism, those in upper castes have bigger homes and servants, because they paid their dues in the last life and now have incarnated at a higher level.

There may be some truth to the link between spirituality and material things. But there are also counter-arguments to this in the monastic traditions. Many religions require vows of poverty. Maybe instead of getting what you want, it is as the Rolling Stones say, "You get what you need." If the mind is very busy focusing on wants it is similar to trying not to feel certain emotions. It keeps the mind closed and not open. Therefore a step towards permanent transformation is to let go of wants.

There is a trick from Fritz Perls (1992), a humanist psychologist. He said that one has to accept things to change them. To apply this to the case in point, not cluttering the mind with wants, one can affirm desires and then let go of them. I try to apply this in my life working for a graduate school. They pay me very well, but it is not enough to save any money. I need to earn $500 more a month to get ready for retirement. So to use Perls' dictum, I can say, "I want $500 more a month," but then immediately release the idea, so that my mind can stay open and not close in on my desires.

DYING TO THE EGO

Early in my journey, I had many misconceptions about what being spiritual was. From the yoga circles I frequented, I knew the New Age dictum that it was bad to "ego out." Dying to the ego was a popular phrase, and I tried my best to accomplish this. I thought this meant not having emotions, or if I did have them I needed to get over them immediately. If someone was insulting me then I thought I should be able to act like it didn't happen. Dying to the ego overlapped with my Christian training of "turning the other cheek." This era of my thinking was around the time I read Ram Dass' book, *The Only Dance There Is*, published in 1974. He described chanting "*Om mani padme hum*"[1] while driving his convertible across North America. However, this didn't completely work to silence his ego as evidenced by his book *Grist for the Mill*, published in 1979. It was obviously not so easy to release the ego's control.

I didn't have much luck either. Maybe it was because I was a fiery red-haired, hazel-eyed woman of Scottish descent. I had many emotions and they didn't go away. I remember a particularly intense time when I was married to a man who inspired me with his non-materialism and high values. We may have been the first adherents to "voluntary simplicity," even though the phrase had not been coined yet. Both highly educated, we chose not to make

---

1   This is a Tibetan Buddhist mantra which means to transform to the wisdom of the jewel of the lotus.

much money and to buy as little as possible. We had no credit cards or debts. I had a 1970 green Volvo from a previous divorce settlement. I got the car, but not the state of the art radio/audio tape system, and because of this I'd been tooling around for years without a radio. Once I was driving to a yoga workshop in the Wilshire area trying to navigate the packed L.A. freeways, while simultaneously reaching over to the passenger's seat tuning a small battery-operated radio. Needless to say my buying abstinence had not simplified my life. On our next road trip we had decided to buy a radio, since it would have been good to listen to some tunes on the way back to Arizona. We checked out car radios at many stores, finally choosing one. Then my husband said, "No, I don't think we need one after all." I was crushed, but immediately thought, "Let go, this is just my ego who wants the radio."

However, I found that I was angry for weeks and couldn't release the feeling. Many years later during therapy, a psychologist told me I needed to learn to say what I wanted. I could have overridden my husband and said, "Sorry, I'm buying it anyway." But at the time I was confused and thought that I could disable my ego's control over my life by not caring. My idea was just to push it down and pretend that it didn't exist. But denial didn't work. As a fear-based entity, the ego creates stability so that a person is not confused or out-of-control. This is good up to a point, but it keeps the mind closed to the unconscious which becomes a fortress of stored memories, sapping energy and denying access.

My experiences showed me that I couldn't "control" emotions and tell my ego to let go. My unconscious would keep erupting with anger or resentment expressing things that were suppressed, and the ego would do its job of trying to keep these things hidden whether or not I wanted it to. It would keep things out of my conscious awareness only to come out later in an uncontrolled way. This didn't seem a very constructive path on my way to wisdom. Trying to be spiritual by trying not to "ego out" wasn't working. I needed something else to open the mind, to make my mind like Patanjali's sky (Prabhu and Bhat 2013).

EMOTIONS

Thank goodness there was help in the form of a psychologist, Takeshi Masui (1987). At a conference in 1987 held in Fukuoka, on Japan's southern island, I heard Masui explain how to heal emotions with imagery. He had us talk about an unpleasant event that had occurred in the recent past, and then find a location in our bodies where we felt it the most. After finding the spot, in the stomach or throat, for example, the next step was to see what the emotion looked like including its color, size, shape, texture and density. The exercise was to create a 3D picture and then to start changing that picture to release the intensity of the emotion. For example, if I saw a black fist clenched in my stomach, then I would give my body permission to change it. In this case, using Masui's technique, I could see the fist unclenching and then the colors change from black to brown to green.

I tried this technique for an experience I had while working at Prescott College in Arizona. I oversaw the process of giving college credit for life experience. One of our students documented his Spanish language skills, and I had a professor at an adjacent Community College evaluate his work and award credit. I would have asked the Prescott College's Spanish professor to evaluate the work first, but he always said he was too busy. He was from Spain and interested in Spanish language literature, such as Don Quixote's stories, and looked down at the community college professors. The Spaniard got wind of the evaluation and went to the President of the college in a furious huff and said that no credit should be awarded. I had acted to protect our academic reputation and at the same time assist the student. I wanted the President to support me. He ignored me, and I was mortified that someone could use misplaced arrogance about rigor to deny a student credit. But I was overruled, and there was not much I could do about it. I thought I'd better use imagery to deal with my anger. Following Masui's instructions, I found the place I felt most about this event. There was a tight knot at the top of my stomach under my rib cage. It was a black ball two inches in diameter. I created a relaxed focus of attention on this image. Then, I kept my attention on the circumference of the ball and softened it, letting the energy dissipate. I saw the color shift from black to brown, and then from yellow to green. The anger I had about the incident went away, and I was able to let it go and make decisions about how I wanted to handle a similar situation in the future. Further, I had made a very small step to restructure my mind so that emotions could come and go like the clouds.

What I learned about emotions and the ego with these experiences was that some actual technique was needed to make my mind whole. Masui's imagery showed me I needed to trick my ego to let go and open the unconscious, and in this case paying attention to a visual image was the key. This laid the foundation for my theory that visualizing an archetype could do the same thing in an even more powerful way.

IMAGERY EXERCISE: EMOTION

Take a few moments and feel yourself move into your body. Make sure your legs are uncrossed, and both feet are on the ground. Put your hands on your legs. Take a deep breath and feel your whole body getting heavier and warmer. Roll your shoulders, moving back, and bring them down slightly. Give your body a firm, positive suggestion to relax. Feel yourself getting heavier and warmer again. Relax your toes in your right foot, your entire leg, see the ball and socket of your right hip, open it slightly with your mind's eye. Relax your toes in your left foot, your entire leg, see the ball and socket of your left hip, open it slightly with your mind's eye. Relax your groin area, your stomach, your heart, your lungs. Relax your right hand, feel a heavy, but not too heavy, ball in your right palm. It is orange, and as you feel it your right hand relaxes. Relax your left hand, feel a heavy, but not too heavy ball, in your left palm. It is blue-green, and as you feel it your left hand relaxes. Your right arm is heavy, as is your left arm. See the ball and socket of your right shoulder joint, open it. See the ball on socket of your left shoulder joint, open it. Go to the small of your back, walk up your vertebrae as if your attention has fingers and restack them. Relax the long muscles on either side of your back. Go to the very top of your vertebrae where your cranium sits. Relax that point. Relax the back of your head, the top. Your cheeks, your lips, your tongue, relax your eyes, your ears. Your whole body is heavier and warmer.

Now think about a time in the past several weeks when you have felt something you didn't like. Imagine it as vividly as you can, as if it is a movie playing in your mind. You are there and it is happening right now. Where are you? Who is there with you? Try to notice some perceptual details. Do you notice colors, textures? Sounds? Give yourself a few minutes and let the image move as it will. (Wait a bit.)

Now where in your body are you feeling something? Do you feel something in the stomach, head, neck, legs, hands, or heart? Empower yourself to notice a sensation. Now take your attention to that spot in your body, and try to visualize it. Pretend that you are watching a cartoon. Or that it is magical. How big is it? What shape? What color? Visualize it as clearly as you can. Do you like it? If not, give yourself permission to change it. You could change colors, change shapes, you can do anything you want with it. Take it out, burn it up, or just gently shift the color from black to green, for example. Let it transform.

Now come out of the imagery. Try to keep the sense that you created.

THE EGO

Humans feel very strong emotions when their sense of stability is threatened. Masui's imagery tools help defuse those emotions, but in the long run if the ego can become more relaxed and not take external events as threatening then the mind can become more subtle, allowing emotions to move through, just as the Dalai Lama does. The ego is a functional part of the mind, not bad or good. Since it is the center of the personality, it has the job of self-preservation. Over time, it seeks coherence, stabilizing the inner world so that a person can take actions for self-advantage. It is the integration point of an individual life. Initially infants and very young children have no sense of themselves or where they start and where they end. Freud notes that the stability function can get out of control. In *An Outline of Psycho-Analysis* he writes, "the more hard-pressed the ego, the convulsively it clings (as though in a fight)...to protect what remains of itself from further eruptions" (Freud 1949, p.35). At any point in the developmental process the ego can get out of control through trauma or other extraordinary events. It becomes hyperactive, narrowing conscious awareness by creating barriers.

The ego avoids sensations and events that are too strong by pushing them out of conscious awareness. For example, if a young child sees his father beat his mother, he first feels fear at the shocking and frightening scene. If this event had been less frightening, such as a newspaper story of a battered wife, there would be no need for this. Instead the ego would keep the information in conscious awareness, letting the child think about ways to be protective in the future. The new information is integrated, not put away out of sight. Over time, these children develop a point of reference to integrate internal and external sensations and events to bring continuity to their life. A strong sense of self encourages the ego to let go.

Psychologists define an integrated ego as being a marker of psychological health. A vivid metaphor for this is the French, "*bien dans sa peau*," saying that people feel comfortable in their own skin. A person's affective world is solid, stable, and internal sensations are organized and coordinated. For example, a person could be angry for one second and then vulnerable the next. The ego acts as a fulcrum to balance these two disparate characteristics. It is like the eye in the storm in the inner world. All around is chaos, but at the center is awareness. A person feels, "I am here. I exist. I am separate from people and events going on outside of me. I remember the past and can speculate on the future."

But no ego is perfectly integrated. A human has many traits that are contradictory. For example, a person can be loving or hateful, shy or aggressive, depending on the situation. This can be crazy-making since a person thinks, "Which one am I?" Most people have parts of the self in conscious awareness and others that are hidden. From the field of interpersonal communication a diagram called the JoHari window explains how conflicting elements can come into conscious view. As the ego becomes secure, more and more of the inner world comes into view. This in turn translates to an integrated ego creating emotional health.

The JoHari window appears as a square divided into four quadrants. The upper left quadrant contains what a person and everyone else knows about the self. In the upper right is what others know about a person but the person doesn't know. In the lower left is what the person knows about him or herself but others don't know, and in the lower right is what is hidden from the self and others. The window represents conscious awareness. At first it is only as big as the upper left quadrant, exposing a small part of the mind. But as the ego becomes strong, it doesn't have to shove so much into the unconscious, and it allows the window to open more and more. Ultimately with emotional maturity the window may even disappear as the mind becomes spacious. Contradictory parts of the self come into view without the ego seeking flight. The entire mind can never be truly open, but the idea is that the unconscious is not sealed up by an insecure ego. This is not only emotional health, but creates a natural continuity to spirituality.

The ego's job is to give coherence by differentiating or separating the sense of "I-ness" from inner and outer events. Initially it is immersed in the wave of experience, but over time it separates itself to gain awareness. As this happens, a human learns to pay attention to certain things, and ignore others. They emerge from the embeddedness of their experience. Certain sensations are pushed into the unconscious, other things are ignored. For example, a child learns to ignore the sound of a train outside and instead pays attention to the mother's voice reading a story. The human becomes more and more selective in focus to eventually disassociate from the ego itself.

If all goes well, humans become more and more sophisticated at doing this. Step by step, he or she grows to be emotionally mature.

Over time a person can differentiate the self from:

- internal sensations, emotions and memories

- incoming perceptions of sight, sound, touch, movement, taste or smell

- mother, father and other family members

- friends and others in the environment

- societal roles and expectations

- internal roles and expectations.

The ego matures from defining itself as a part of events, people, roles, inner tapes, expectations, emotions and perceptions. Inner awareness becomes linked to present time: "I exist here and now." This differentiation can even progress towards spiritual maturity. The ego helps people realize that they are different than the world, and this process eventually leads to a realization that the ego is not the same as the self. Freud wrote that the ego is an unavoidable detour to achieve peace, since humans need stability before letting go into the unknown. A person with a relaxed ego can handle upsetting events with a certain level of resiliency. The person can also be flexible. Certain ideas or emotions can be strong, but this person can let go of them or gain perspective.

If people separate themselves from inner thoughts and emotions, and create a wise mind, they can see themselves more clearly. I knew a man who was very insecure and saw himself as a social misfit, based on some unfortunate early events in his childhood. He did not realize that he was a charming, socially adept person with great qualities. I also knew a woman who thought of herself as overly polite, but she would say the most glaring, potentially insulting things once in a while. This always came as a shock when she heard obtuse comments erupting from her mouth. It seemed to be her way of releasing anxiety. If both of these people gained the ability to separate their sense of who they were from their inner experience, their hidden parts would be revealed creating a more integrated sense of self. The young man could be more confident, and the woman could be aware that she could easily blurt out an inappropriate remark and censure herself more easily. These examples reinforce the idea that integration is possible through the differentiation of the self from experience, which is what the ego is designed to do.

RELAXING AND DISTRACTING THE EGO

After my earlier attempts at dying to my ego failed, I started learning how to relax or at least distract it. Hindu philosophy ignores the ego and prescribes holding the attention on something instead of working with the ego directly. Inner focus prompts a stable center in the mind. As the mind is trained to focus attention, the unconscious naturally opens up. Internal sensations and memories come and go and suppressed material in the unconscious is released. On the other hand, Western psychological therapy encourages people to get in touch with their emotions and express them by creating a safe therapeutic environment to strengthen the ego. A strong ego in turn relaxes and prompts the unconscious to open.

Even though these paths are different, the outcome is the same. A relaxed ego differentiates itself from memories, sensations and emotions, and this translates to a healthy, potentially wise human being. But it is important to note the difference in the paths of Western psychology and Hindu philosophy. The Western approach is to develop a strong ego, while the other avenue is to create a sophisticated focus which disables the ego. I translate this latter method into a Western-friendly approach, of using a human's natural fascination with an archetype as a means of developing this focus. As a result, the ego is distracted and doesn't fight to maintain control.

STEPS TO RELAXING THE EGO

Relaxing the ego takes time and has ups and downs as consciousness changes to become roomier and less restricted. Inner transformation may follow these steps, which are more like a dynamic spiral, moving in and out, instead of in a linear progression. The inner experience of the mind changes as the unconscious is opened and the ego becomes more relaxed. Instead of rigidity of black or white thinking, or a state of anxiety with circulating insecurities, or of focusing on negative events and blaming others, the mind becomes more spacious through the following progression:

- *Denial.* At first the ego is firmly in control, and anything uncomfortable is relegated to the unconscious. A human has a rigid reality of what is good and bad. However, once in a while there is emotional upheaval, creating inner chaos and a sense that things are not as good as they seem.

- *Choice.* A person decides to wake up and become spiritual. There is a sense of a different way of being and a yearning to be more calm and loving. Usually a person adopts some spiritual practices at this point, such as yoga, meditation or church attendance. These begin to have an effect, and periodically a person feels bliss, as well as peace and calm. But these states do not last, and sometimes they are followed by depression.

- *Certainty.* As a person chooses to adopt spiritual practices, he or she can experience blissful highs. Confidence and a feeling of superiority emerge over time. A person thinks, "This is it. Spirituality is achieved." But problems arise and emotions rage. Things don't go the right way. Out of highs come lows. One realizes that superiority of any kind inhibits the changes needed.

- *Difficulty.* This tension prompts change. Becoming spiritual is not a one-shot event. It happens over time with small, subtle events. Problems occur, and a person realizes that the path is more difficult and deeper than initially conceived. But not all is lost: it can be a positive shift, one of humility. A person cannot create spirituality within by being "right" or being in "control." Rather, surrendering is the key.

- *Acceptance.* The continual cycle of certainty and difficulty brings one to acceptance of whatever occurs inside. Buddhists say, "Accept what is." The psychologists say, "You have to accept something before it changes." This attitude creates strengthened humility, the next step for sustained spirituality.

- *Allowing.* Acceptance gives way to allowing. If the mind is like the sky, then the storm clouds with continuous lightning give way to blue skies. Whatever happens inside comes and goes.

- *Subtlety.* Over time, the mind becomes airy, and it is distributed evenly across a large space, and it has a radiance that glows. There are ups and downs, but there is constancy beneath it all.

Noting the shifts in one's consciousness can give confidence in the transformation. Those who become wise can have a profound, subtle effect on others around them.

ARCHETYPES, EGO AND EMOTIONS

It is complicated and difficult to change the mind so that it becomes spacious and ultimately wise. A direct method has risks since the ego will fight in its need for control. However, as the ego is relaxed, there is more space for awareness. An insult does not result in anger. Instead an internal dialogue can take place: "I don't need to react." If the person used Masui's technique of finding the feeling of the emotion in the body, imaging it, the ego allows the release. It is indirect and may seem counterintuitive, but it is highly effective. Learning how the ego operates gives clarity that relaxing or distracting it will allow the mind to open and eventually become wise. The ego has its job, and emotions are good messages of things to pay attention to; but to have a consistent experience of peace and joy, a changed mind can keep them from taking over.

CHAPTER 4

IMAGERY TO OPEN THE MIND

Up to this chapter, I've been setting groundwork for how archetypal imagery will change the inner world for wisdom. I've documented the spiritual quest that has become a cultural phenomenon and how psychological and spiritual models of the mind lead to a method of transformation. A slight detour showed what a difficult process this is since the ego is set up to keep awareness out of the unconscious. There is a form of thinking that naturally "talks" to the unconscious and that is seeing pictures or images in the mind. In this chapter I review the brain research on the process of imagery to show how it can be a powerful tool to open the unconscious.

THE AMAZING BRAIN

Neurophysiologists Richard Restak (2010), creator of the PBS series *The Brain*, has explained humans' amazing inner capacity. Restak showed that the sheer volume of what happens in the mind is breathtaking. There are over 100 trillion neural connections in the brain, more than there are known stars in the universe. Humans are born with many, many brain cells. Different sources cite different numbers, but two million might be a good guess. The miracle of the brain is that new neural connections can grow, adding to the size and potential of the brain. Thinking in pictures can help people use more of their brains.

Another scientist helped underscore the importance of imagery, expanding the possibilities of what the brain could do.

Her name was Jeanne Achterberg (1985), and I heard her speak at a conference in New York City in 1988. It was one of those vivid memories, signifying a life-changing event. I entered a large meeting room in an old hotel. The ceiling had decorative molding with a few paint chips coming off. As I took my seat, Achterberg was flipping through slides showing paintings with vivid colors, as well as pictures of the human immune system. She was a psychologist at a Texas hospital's cancer unit where her M.D. colleagues called her a witch doctor since they didn't believe in what she did. They only gave her patients who were near death. However, she fooled them by helping hopeless cases survive and living to tell about it. She taught them imagery to increase their white blood cell counts and shrink their tumors. To her, imagery was a powerful tool to unleash human potential locked in the unconscious.

I believed Achterberg's proposition because of an experience with my nephew around the same time. He had lymphoma and had been hospitalized because of his very low white blood cell counts. His doctor was afraid that any infection, even a cold, could be harmful. I visited him in his hospital room and asked if he wanted to try imagery. He was enthusiastic, so I had him direct his attention to the femur in the middle of his thigh, the largest bone in the body. He imagined that the bone marrow there was manufacturing thousands of white blood cells. At the age of thirteen he enjoyed video games, so he visualized white soldiers coming out of his bone marrow in droves and swimming into the blood stream. The next day he was released from the hospital because his blood tests showed an increase in these immunity cells. This was not a scientific study, but he felt that something had happened. He was able to open his unconscious mind with imagery and increase his white blood cells. The unconscious had been made conscious.

IMAGERY AND BRAIN WAVES

When the brain experiences different states of consciousness, it emits certain brain waves. Researchers have documented four primary ones: alpha, beta, theta and delta. Alpha denotes waking with a relaxed focus of attention, while beta is an alert consciousness consistent with "getting things done" energy. Theta is an expanded, creative dream-like state, sometimes accompanied by a sense of being interconnected with all of life and sometimes feelings of bliss or peace (Wise 1995). The most noticeable theta state happens during the drowsy period right before sleep when consciousness erupts with flashes of images, or when meditators report seeing their guru's face. The fourth brain wave, delta, occurs in deep sleep. It is obviously important, because without it humans cannot restore, but it is not a state that can be consciously evoked.

The highs of spiritual experience are most closely associated with theta waves. These could happen during the visions that accompany mystics' transformations or scientists' breakthroughs. For example, Tesla, the genius who invented the alternating current motor, saw his discovery in a flash of light, and then he visualized how to build the device.

I'm no Tesla but, sometimes, I've had waking visions in the wilderness or meditating during yoga deep relaxation. Once when camping at the base of the San Francisco Peaks near Flagstaff, Arizona, I saw mudheads, one of the Hopi tribe's spirits or katsinas (Walters 1977) hiding behind the trees. These spirits had spherical heads covered by dried mud and crowned with feathers. They looked out from behind trees and laughed at me, acting in their true trickster nature. When I have had visions like this I experience great joy, but also have confusion and questions. Sometimes I feel like Kevin Costner in the movie *Field of Dreams.* A voice told him to build the baseball field, but he didn't know why. He followed his heart and ended up on a good path, but he was very confused during the process. The spiritual path is like that, ambiguous, giving only one step at a time. These events are often messages from the spirit world, and the meaning or the recommended actions are not immediately evident.

Another time, I attended the Transpersonal Psychology Conference in the Asilomar Conference Center on the oceanfront of Monterrey Bay. It was a magical location. I could hear seals bark at night and surf crash on the beach. In the 1980s, I often found myself lying on the floor with eyes shut, hearing drumming or trance music while listening to visualization instructions. In this specific case, a man was telling us to see an animal emerge from each chakra.[1] I could see the animals in great detail, and at the end I visualized them all coming together to give us advice. At my base chakra I had seen a rattlesnake. This gripped me since snakes are the symbol of the kundalini energy curled at the bottom of the spine. Yogis say that if this is awakened, all the chakras will open through the crown at the top of the head, burning up the barrier to the unconscious mind. Later that day, I was at the conference bookstore, drawn to a book with a rattlesnake on the cover. The snake looked exactly the same as the one in my visions. I took it as an auspicious sign that I was on the right path. Like Kevin Costner, I got the message, but I didn't know what it meant. It did give me a feeling of grace, though. Imagery for me became a tool for exploding the barriers in the mind to make the unconscious conscious. I studied this phenomenon for many years.

Theta experiences aren't always visions because sometimes they are just huge emotions that change a person's worldview, clearing out the mind. A case in point was St. Francis' awakening to the spiritual life. After returning to Italy ill from the Crusades, St. Francis awoke with a sense of wonderment at all that he saw. As depicted in Zeffirelli's 1972 movie *Brother Sun, Sister Moon*, St. Francis climbed out of his mosquito netting clad in a sheer, gauze nightshirt, surrounded by whitewashed walls, ivory candles, and seeing praying nuns wearing cream-colored habits. With eyes burning bright he heard the chirp of a bird outside his chamber. Attempting to find its source, he climbed outside his window, high in a tower of his father's mansion. As he balanced on the edge of the roof, he basked in the bird's beauty. He realized that creation was miraculous and that focusing on money and prestige was a distraction. He then ran to his father's store house of imported fabrics and threw the riches out the window for the poor. His theta experience changed his consciousness, allowing him to value life above material things.

Another famous theta story is described by Ramakrishna (Vivekananda 1956) who was Vivekananda's teacher, the

---

1   The seven Hindu energy centers starting at the base of the spine and moving out the top of the head.

philosopher who brought Hinduism to the west in 1902 at the Parliament of Religions in Chicago. Ramakrishna described a vision which radically changed his worldview. When he was in the presence of a statue of the Hindu goddess Kali, he saw her as a huge, earth mother radiating golden light filling him with such brilliant and vigorous love that he was thrown to the floor. Needless to say he became a lifelong devotee of Kali. Other spiritual practitioners recall similar overwhelming emotional experiences. But usually they are not permanently transformed. This leads to the question of the role of theta experiences in sustained spirituality.

For the great masters, theta visions seem to permanently transform their consciousness. But for mere mortals, theta states occur, but the next day can present anger or frustration at the people and situations around us. More commonly, the highs come and go but a sustained spiritual state escapes us.

Jean Houston (1997, 2000), a psychologist, has a metaphor to understand the purpose of these theta highs. Readers may remember how she helped Hillary Clinton cope with Bill's infidelity. She directed Hillary to visualize conversations with her idol, Eleanor Roosevelt. Houston, an expert on opening the unconscious, proposes that some experiences act as "depth charges" from the spiritual realm or what I call the energy field. Visions and ecstatic experiences are such explosions, and over time they can expand the mind by making the barriers to the unconscious more permeable. Theta highs are important since they evoke experiences of transcendence, giving a taste of permanent transformation. But other practices are the real key to ongoing spirituality, particularly creating alpha waves.

Most people aren't spiritual masters like Vivekananda or St. Francis. Their minds aren't permanently transformed to a spiritual reality with one major theta experience. However, learning to create alpha waves can subtly open the inner world toward spaciousness over time. It is not just a matter of concentrating, but relaxing at the same time. Visualization[2] creates a relaxed focus

---

2   I use 'imagery' and 'visualization' interchangeably. Technically, though, imagery is creating internal experiences across any of the five senses: auditory, visual, kinesthetic, tactile or olfactory. Visualization uses only the visual mode.

and as a result generates alpha waves. Biofeedback practices show this. If people think in words to change their blood pressure, it doesn't work. Worrying about how high the meter reads, or trying very hard to lower it, doesn't affect the gauge. But thinking in pictures has the opposite effect and relaxes tension in blood vessels. To lower blood pressure, one could imagine floating in a beautiful pool of turquoise water and rocking gently in the water. It is a different process to think in pictures instead of words, since it opens the unconscious, creating alpha waves which automatically lower the blood pressure.

The story about changing blood pressure by picturing oneself floating in a warm pool shows that the mind and body are not separated. Fixating attention in the body is effective in changing physiology once thought to be outside of conscious control. Similarly, it can be a tool to make lasting changes in the inner world to open the mind to other domains.

ATTITUDES FOR IMAGERY

Practicing visualization can create alpha waves and become a powerful tool on the wisdom path. A few basic attitudes can increase imagery skills.

Attitude 1: Accepting what is inside…and outside

Accepting the inner world helps create vivid images. Many people want to see pictures a certain way, and worry about whether or not they are doing the right thing. But allowing whatever comes up without judgment is the key. "Accepting what is" has many benefits. The mind is often besieged with thoughts evaluating one's self and internal emotions. Much internal conflict is about positioning oneself in relation to an emotion. The mind chatter asks, "Is this a good one or a bad one?" Or it says, "I shouldn't feel this." Sometimes the turmoil does not come to conscious awareness, but it is shoved into the unconscious without recognition. A meditation technique of watching what is going on inside helps diffuse it by thinking something like "Oh, I'm having that thought now." This is more helpful than trying to evaluate, stop or change it. Sometimes it will then disappear like the clouds in Patanjali's sky model of the mind (Satchidananda 2012). The clouds drift across the sky, with no attachment to anyone. A cornerstone of this approach is that resistance is futile since it just feeds what one wants.

Many meditation techniques use the idea of watching what is going on inside and not engaging with it. This has a similar effect as acceptance. The emotion is there but there is nothing to do about it or any judgment to make. Of course, this is easier said than done. I think many assume that they can control what is inside, as opposed to allowing it to exist. However, with control the thoughts and emotions get bigger and more intense, or else they are pushed into the unconscious, building up pressure towards a later explosion. The ticket here is acceptance of whatever comes up with gentleness.

Acceptance can be applied to outside events as well. Life often deals people happiness, sadness, surprises, boredom, tragedy and many other unwanted events. Many people argue with what happens to them, becoming a modern-day Job: "Why me, God?" In these scenarios a person can end up fighting with what is happening around them. But things can go much more smoothly if one can say, "I don't like this, this isn't fair. I feel a lot of pain." But simultaneously say, "I accept what is." This doesn't mean that a person feels good about what's happening. It is not easy and takes patience to wait with the unease, but it is actually in a person's self-interest since it decreases suffering. All in all, "accepting what is," or at least choosing to do this, will increase a person's happiness and transform the mind.

Attitude 2: Be willing to have internal chaotic states

After accepting what is, the next attitude to adopt is to realize that it can get pretty dicey inside as the ego becomes relaxed and suppressed memories and emotions come out. All that humans experience or feel is stored in this memory bank. When a person on the sacred path chooses to let go of the ego's control of reality, a huge amount of material trapped there can rush out.

As mentioned earlier, Stanislav Grof (1989) detailed how at certain points people experience what might be termed an emergency. They feel crazy inside with a sense that they are splitting apart, similarly to what St. John of the Cross describes in his poem *The Dark Night of the Soul*. They can be filled with pain and despair. According to the theologians, difficult times are to be expected on the spiritual path. Out of these dark periods comes a new plateau.

I've had many experiences like this. I talked about one in my book, *Living the Wheel: Working with Emotions, Terror and Bliss with Imagery* (Nelson 1993). In the book, I told the story of being in a Buddhist temple in Tokyo and having the shakes. It was greatly unexpected since I thought I was just intellectually interested in meditation and Eastern philosophy. Then my heart felt like the heavens opened and filled it up, which was a very unsettling experience. As people refine their imagery skills, they can hold a focus even during inner confusion and chaos. It takes a change in attitude to accept these experiences as something that will help transform to spirituality.

Attitude 3: Trust the Self

The ego creates a sense of stability, and as the mind relaxes, it may feel like one is drifting. But trusting that there is a spiritual Self will help map uncharted waters. I remember a story from a mother who was a psychologist and raised three children. She thought she knew what to expect with her third child. However, each child was different and found new ways to push the buttons inside. One of her children had been the sweetest child, very agreeable and one who liked to please. But in the teenage years, she became quite rude and would insult her mom. The daughter would contradict anything she said, and if the daughter was questioned then the mom became the horrible person. This came as a surprise, even though as a psychologist she knew it was bound to happen. Teenagers need to individuate, or prove that they are functioning adults outside their parents' supervision. Finally, the mother admitted that she was having a difficult time coping with the emotional charges awakened by a mouthy teenager, so she decided to go to another psychologist for a tune-up. She thought she needed at least five sessions, so she made herself go that many times even if the predictable resistance to the therapist reared its head. During the fifth session, the therapist said, "You can't change the person, and you know the person is not going to change." The mom decided she wasn't going to change what happened around her or be able to deny it either. She had to trust in some other force besides her ego's hold on reality to help her be flexible and handle the inner turmoil of emotions. She let go of the illusion of ego stability. She couldn't control other people and how they interacted with her. The world and people in her life were outside of her command. Acquiescing kept her mind soft on the path to wisdom.

The following imagery exercises can give a taste of the experience, which naturally creates relaxation and opens the unconscious. I encourage practitioners to try them before doing them with clients. The first one is designed to create profound relaxation. The second prompts a person to visualize an animal.

IMAGERY EXERCISE: RELAXATION

Take your attention to your body. Start with the right toes. Relax each toe, big one, second, third, fourth and little toe. Take your attention to the very tip of the toes. Try to imagine the cells on the very end that are ready to flake off. Relax your right foot, ankle, calf, go underneath the knee cap. Relax the quadriceps, the biggest muscle in your body. Open your right hip. Now go down to the left toes, big, second, middle, third and little. Relax the whole foot, left ankle, calf, knee, under the kneecap, left quadriceps, open the left hip. Take your attention to the lower back and pretending that your attention has fingers walk up slowly through your vertebrae, starting at the base of the spine, moving up one by one. Imagine you are stacking up the joints and visualizing space between them. Relax the long muscles on each of side of your back. Take your attention to your right hand. See a yellow-orange ball in the palm of your hand. It is heavy. Relax each finger, pinky, ring, middle, index and thumb. Relax your lower arm, elbow and upper arm. Open your right shoulder. See a blue-green ball in your left hand. It is heavy and it relaxes your palm. Relax your pinky, ring, middle, index and thumb. Relax your left forearm, elbow and upper arm. Open your left shoulder joint. Relax the back of your neck and go up to the point where your cranium sits on your neck. Open that space. Relax the back of your head, the top of your head. Unlock your jaw, relax your lips, make your cheeks and nose flat. Open your third eye. Feel the lobes of your ears grow longer. Feel your whole body becoming warm and heavy. Take your attention to your heart and thank it for beating 24 hours a day. Feel your heart growing larger, stronger and warmer.

IMAGERY EXERCISE: ANIMAL HELPER

Imagine that you are outside in a place that you have been before. It could be in your backyard, or on a boat in the ocean, or on the beach... Imagine that it is playing right now in your mind's eye like a movie in present time. Vivify all your senses. What do you see right in front of you: a tree, the mast of a sailor, the ocean lapping near you? Notice colors, the green of the trees, the soft white of the clouds. Then reach out and touch something, the leaves hanging down, or the sand on the beach, or the smooth wood of a beam. What does it feel like? Move in this setting, see what it feels like to walk, which part of your body of your body is moving? Smell. Do you smell the fresh air in the wind, is it full of humidity, does it smell of the earth, or does it have the aroma of a pine tree? What do you hear? A bird, the sound of the waves, the wind in the trees? Vivify this. Be there, make it as if it is happening now.

You are feeling okay. Not too happy, nor sad, but just okay. There is nothing to do, no one is depending on you. You are just with yourself right now.

Find a spot where it feels okay to sit down and rest for a bit. You imagine that a positive entity is coming to you. Possibly it is an animal. It is not a scary animal. It may be a wild animal, but it means you no harm.

Imagine that the animal is coming to you. It makes you happy in your heart to see this animal coming. Again, notice the perceptual details. Feathers, fur, size, color. Take a moment and let the animal come to you in this outside place that feels good to you. What do you notice about the animal, what stands out for you when you look at it, a color, or a movement? Does the animal say anything to you or have a message? Where in your body do you feel something and how would you describe it? Is it warm, do you feel happiness or sadness? Come back to this time and space. Keep this feeling.

Imagery is a powerful tool to change the mind to spaciousness. If a person learned to image well there would be many benefits. Physical health would be optimized since imagery communicates to the immune system. The mind would be more relaxed, making room for both rational thought and intuitive insights. Suppressed memories from the unconscious could move up and out, creating more peace and wellbeing.

CHAPTER 5

POWER OF ARCHETYPES

Visualizing archetypes can be a powerful tool for transforming the mind. An archetype is a collection of characteristics that form a recognizable pattern, residing in the energetic domain. Examples are a sports hero, a seductress movie star, a martyr or a criminal. From a psychological position, archetypes motivate human behavior in the following way. An individual's ego identifies with an archetype to organize its personality and motivate action. This process is evident when watching young children playing. When I'm sitting in a park, I can see primal patterns being enacted. One child helps another one stand up after a fall—a future healer or hero. Another child is being a bully, a future villain, and another is performing feats of daring on the play equipment, a future sports star or hero.

Practices, knowledge and attitudes combine to a make a powerful arsenal to transform the mind to spaciousness. Imaging an archetype is a key skill to realize this. Archetypes make the change process easier since they tap the mind's natural workings. They reside in the energy field in the unconscious, and at the same time are connected to the ego in the conscious. Archetypes lighten the load of the spiritual path since one can use intuition and a playful mode to find them. There is not a specific set of archetypes, nor a magical list to choose from. Power animals given by a shaman, such as a bear, coyote, whale or eagle, are not exclusive. Nor is the list of Greek deities such as those in Jean Shinoda Bolen's (2004) book, *Goddesses in Everywoman: Powerful Archetypes in Women's Lives*. It doesn't matter which archetype one chooses, and the choice can change as the intuition guides. A person can stay with an archetype as long as the fascination is there, and let go of one, making room for another at any time. Marie-Louise von Franz (1985), a renowned Jungian writer, explains that each archetype contains every other one. One can experiment and try out different ones.

One of my colleagues, Judy Stevens Long (2000), has a theory about psychological development that an emotionally mature person has an ego like a prism. A person's internal lens has different facets changing focus depending on the situation, showing flexibility. The facet idea is similar to von Franz's view of archetypes. Each face of the lens could be a different archetype, but focusing on any one of them creates a window to open the mind. One needn't worry too much about getting the correct archetype. They can come and go, since they all lead to the same place. Not trying too hard and being playful will help the archetype search.

Even though archetypes have a strong unconscious effect on humans, most people are unaware that they are being influenced by them. Archetypes usually operate on the unconscious level. If people can become aware of how the unconscious controls behavior, then they can have more choice and awareness about their actions. They can choose to develop spiritually for example, instead of being controlled by energies erupting from the unconscious. People sometimes wonder why very important people jeopardize their careers by doing stupid things like shoplifting or having an affair. These seemingly aberrant behaviors are no mysteries to psychologists. Something is going on in the unconscious outside of conscious awareness, which results in behaviors that are not in the person's best interest.

One of the first archetypes that impressed me was Ganesha, the elephant-headed Hindu deity that represents new beginnings and the remover of obstacles. When I taught graduate education students in India on a Fulbright, he became very important.

GANESHA'S STORY

From many years of yoga classes, I knew about Ganesha and the fact that Hindus evoked him at the beginning of new ventures, and that he was thought to grace the supplicant with money, food, household goods or any needed material items. He was usually depicted with garlands of flowers flowing over his shoulders, and bronze pots of food and gems at his feet. When I taught in India, I carried his postcard picture in the money pouch that lay against my belly under my waistband. His energy helped me fend off beggars who surrounded me in the streets holding crying, emaciated babies as their hands found my money. I hoped his image would keep my rupees, passports and credit cards near and dear. Plus I just liked him, since he was a stocky, happy soul with a warm heart who could reach out and help me.

I dreamed of him, too. Nights were not always filled with sleep in India. I'd be lying on my rock-hard pallet listening to the droning ceiling fan and the sound of mosquitoes buzzing in my ear, my body damp with layers of moisture from the pregnant humidity. Then I would see him, Ganesha, a huge, golden being. He would be floating in the corner of the room. I was joyful at this vision and started to ask him for help.

My family and I had a hard time getting food. It was expected that we would hire a bearer to buy food and a cook to make local dishes. Also we were to stock our kitchen with a "mixi" which ground dhal to make delicious food such as masala dosas or flat savory pancakes. However, being both broke and egalitarian, it was very hard to do this. In order to get food, one of us would ride a bicycle about a mile in the sweltering heat to buy tomatoes, broccoli and potatoes. To supplement the vegetables on the way home from teaching, I would jump out of a rickshaw at an open-air store and push in front of the Indian locals to get cheese or bread that did not really seem like cheese or bread. I also would get up at 6:00 am each morning to stand in line to buy a plastic baggy of buffalo milk. It was all very strange and difficult, and my two children, aged thirteen and fifteen, and I were often hungry. Desperate, I thought I'd ask Ganesha to remove obstacles for getting food. After such requests, our neighbors would extend a dinner invitation, or my colleague, who lived not too far away, would invite us for tea accompanied by fried savories. Needless to say, this elephant-headed god grew in importance to me.

In the Hindu pantheon, there are three main gods: Vishnu, the preserver; Brahmin, the unknowable; and Shiva, the destroyer.

Shiva had a wife, Parvati, and they had a beautiful son, Ganesha. The father was quite amorous, frequently pursuing his consort. Once she was taking a bath and asked her son to stand guard to protect her from advances (see Figure 5.1). Not appreciating the defense, Shiva became furious and cut off his son's head. Parvati was very angry and demanded that he get a new head for their son. A servant was sent to get the first one he could find and came back with an elephant's head which was placed on Ganesha's body. Through this transformation, he became the elephant god, one of the most beloved deities in India and the remover of obstacles, as elephants can clear logs for new roads. He became the bringer of beneficence as elephants carry great loads of gifts. By losing his head, he gained much.

Figure 5.1 Ganesha, original painting by Ted Garcia
Ganesha is waiting at his mother's bath to protect
her before Shiva comes to behead him.

This story has pertinent lessons. First, it hurts to lose a head. It is not an easy job to soften the ego's control over reality and the process is painful, just as when the human prince's head was ripped off. But there are amazing benefits to the surrender. In Ganesha's case, he gained the power to give bounty to others and to be worshiped by millions. It is hard for a person to lose their ego, or more aptly lose the self-identification with the ego, but the benefits are mighty. When the identification is lost, one's mind can stay open.

AVALOKITESHVARA'S STORY

Another archetype became important to me when I lived in India. I had first heard about the archetype Avalokiteshvara when one of my students returned from trekking in Nepal and pulled her Toyota truck into my gravel driveway in the woods near Prescott, Arizona. As I walked out of the house to meet her, she was sitting on the tailgate of her Toyota truck beaming blissfully. She stuck out her hand with a gift. It was a picture of a Tibetan Buddhist deity, Avalokiteshvara. Marked by rose, orange and turquoise hues, the deity had ten heads, symmetrically placed on top of each other, and had ten thousand arms, splayed above his head like a fan. Turning the picture over, I read the chronicle of his life. He became enlightened and took the bodhisattva vow, promising not to cross over to nirvana until all sentient beings were enlightened. He worked with the poorest of the poor trying to relieve suffering, lifting up those who fell from carrying heavy loads on their heads. There were too many of them to help, and he became overcome with helplessness and loss. His devastation was so profound that his head broke into many pieces, and his spirit was transported to the Buddha's presence. He was put back together again with ten thousand arms and ten heads giving him great capacity.

Avalokiteshvara's ego was bound to his spirituality since he thought he was supposed to do all the work alone. But when he finally let go in despair, he realized that there was a part of him connected to all others in the spiritual domain. He didn't need to do the work alone. He had found his internal spiritual Self which was boundless and beyond his ego.

It is frightening to let go of the ego since it seems like one is hanging out in boundless infinity. But Avalokiteshvara's story shows that there is something more to guide one to a new stability. It is not a literal, concrete reality, but a more diffuse one connected to the energy domain.

Figure 5.2 Ancient mural of Avalokiteshvara, deity of compassion, with his hand extended. He is sometimes depicted without all his arms

ANOTHER ARCHETYPE, VAJRASATTVA

After finding Sophia as my archetype when she appeared in a story I made up, I worked with her for many years. I found stories, books and pictures and tried to write about her. But that was difficult since she is the blueprint of the material world, primordial and even non-verbal. I wanted to spread the word that this archetype could help people meet their spiritual goals. But I was having problems publishing the insights she gave me, which didn't seem fair. This was a joke on me, though, since I knew the spiritual path was not about getting my desires. For many years, I had tried to publish articles and even a fiction book about her entitled *Sophia's Tales*. It was about a modern-day woman named Sophia, who spontaneously shape-shifted into deities such as Isis, the Egyptian goddess of power, Gaia, the Greek goddess of earth's creation, and even Ganesha.

I did all the requisite research, looking at *Writer's Market* to get an agent and writing endless query letters, with no luck. Several agents read it but no one picked it up. At the same time, since I had done years of research about Sophia, I was writing non-fiction academic, psychological articles about her. One of my sources said she was like a red thread ever-present in history but difficult to find. I was beginning to agree with her. Finally, I was able to use Sophia as an example of an archetype in my article on the spacious mind published in *Humanistic Psychology*. I felt triumphant that I was finally able to write about her. But needless to say she was a difficult entity, and I was ready for a new archetype.

In 2003, I was doing a workshop for Fielding Graduate University. It was at a hotel in Alexandria, Virginia, in a generic meeting room. It had no windows, and the air-conditioning was either too cold or non-existent. During an imagery exercise, I led the group to visualize going to an outside setting where they had been before and that they liked. My instructions included feeling pleasant but not too happy or not too sad, just okay. I told them to notice the perceptual details around them. The key to leading successful imagery exercises is to prompt people to pay attention to their sensations. To accomplish this, I suggested that they notice the color of leaves, the wind, and the touch of a twig as they reached out to it. I further directed them to anticipate that a being was coming to join them. My plan was to help them use their intuition to find an archetype.

As I was leading the exercises, I was creating the pictures in my mind. It is my trick to make sure my instructions are vivid. If I could see it in my mind's eye and describe it, then I could be more effective in helping the participants have a powerful experience. In my visualization, I was up in the mountains in Arizona, amidst ancient Ponderosa Pines. I saw an entity peeking out from a tree, just as when I had seen mudhead katsinas years before. But it wasn't a Hopi spirit. As it emerged from the tree, I noticed it was very brown. I had seen his picture and remembered his name, Vajrasattva, a Tibetan deity. Seeing him gave me a great sense of peace, playfulness and joy. I was elated to have found a new archetype.

Just like Sophia that I talked about in Chapter 2, this archetype had come spontaneously through my intuition, and he similarly opened up a new world to me. I remembered his picture from the book *Tantra in Tibet* (Dalai Lama *et al.* 1977). When I got home after the workshop, I jumped to my bookshelf and found the book, flipping through the pages to find the reminiscent image. Looking out from the pages was my new archetype, Vajrasattva, and it began my 12-month quest to learn all about him. I found images and mantras on the Internet. When I went to see the resident Tibetan Buddhist nun in Flagstaff, Arizona, she had a book opened to his picture and mantra on her dining room table. This was a nice synchronicity, giving me assurance that this was the one for me right now. I found out that the objects in his hands were symbolic. He held a bell (the female) and a vajra (the male). He signified the unitive energy of the universe before it was subdivided into opposites, and he was the basic spiritual energy of creation. He was familiar to me, and he had great resonance, just as Sophia had, since his energy was familiar. I had always tried to experience the fundamental energy that underlay our creation, and here he was. He gave me peace and security in myself. Soon after this event, I was in Colorado at my house in Nederland. I went to Boulder and found a Tibetan store, buying a statue of Vajrasattva, and he became my companion for meditation. It made me happy to find him and the following mantra online.

The hundred-syllable mantra of Vajrasattva[1]

OM is the seed syllable that symbolizes the divine vajra body, that is, the holy body of an enlightened being. The

---

[1] In Tibetan Buddhism this mantra would be used with religious restrictions. For the purposes of this book, Vajrasattva is presented as a psychological archetype, and the mantra gives a sense of this archetype's characteristic of oneness.

vajra body is union-oneness with divine vajra speech and mind. At present, your body, speech and mind function separately, but when you attain the enlightened state of Heruka Vajrasattva your divine body, speech, and mind will function simultaneously.

(Yeshe and Ribush 2004, p.261)

FINDING AN ARCHETYPE

Archetypes come to people intuitively and this process can be accelerated by consciously choosing to find one. A person can say something like, "I want an archetype to help me transform my mind to spirituality." Intention works in unpredictable ways, and the next step may be to wait and stop trying. But patience and ambiguity can be rewarded. A vision may come. A picture in a book may strike one's attention while strolling through a store or an image could capture one's fancy on an Internet search. A playful attitude helps the quest, since the ego will not take it too seriously and thus will let down its guard. Little does the ego know that the archetype may ultimately be its demise since it will open the unconscious to diffuse its hold. It doesn't matter which archetype is chosen, since each is like a facet of a prism. They all lead to the Self.

Intuition is the way to find an archetype. There are attitudes and behaviors that help. The first one is choice. One says, "Yes, I can trust my inner sense." The second one is learning to open the mind and to wait for insight. This includes cultivating and tolerating the ambiguity of not knowing. The unconscious does not operate in a linear, logical manner. When one opens an ear to the Self, there is not a straight answer. For example, a person might be asking for divine guidance about how to handle a conflict with a co-worker. Using intuition, and hoping to open to insights, one would first trust, and then wait for it. The third thing to remember is to listen to the body. People often say, "I have a gut feeling." The body sense is a powerful tool for sustained spirituality. One can trust the body much more than the mind when it comes to intuition. A great example of this is when I come out of a store and have forgotten where I parked the car. If I trust my body to walk in the right direction, I usually do, as opposed to trying to figure it out.

I am not saying that intuition is more important than logical thought. But there is a special type of awareness that comes from insight which helps the mind open and become more spacious. Many of us have seen blissful New Age adherents whose message is to rely on the feeling versus the rational or tout the popularity of the right hemisphere. This is silly since humans have two hemispheres and both are needed. Humans' rational minds are quite important in science, in setting up plans and in verifying information. The real key is to empty the mind so that it is spacious. As this happens, intuition and rationality can work together as needed. The logic continues, the words come and go, and simultaneously insights present themselves.

A person can choose to work consciously with an archetype for both psychological and spiritual development. Ways of working with one include finding stories, writing stories, drawing or visualizing the personification. The simplest way to begin is to find a picture and a story. Archetypes which are deities are particularly powerful since they have a spiritual dimension. Because of the fundamental role of imagery in human cognition, imaging an archetype is a natural and effective way to transform the mind for peace and joy.

Finding an archetype through imagery could be the beginning of an encounter led by intuition. Synchronicity or meaningful coincidences may follow. Without forethought, a person could end up visiting a friend and find a book of poems on the coffee table about the chosen archetype. Identification with an archetype is an avenue towards a spacious, wise mind. In the next day or two make some notes. See where it leads.

CHAPTER 6

MAJOR TAROT ARCHETYPES FOR EMOTIONAL HEALTH

One source for finding an archetype is to look at tools that humans have used for centuries. This chapter presents archetypes from the tarot. People have turned to tarot decks for revealing deep mysteries for centuries. The tarot is a deck of 78 cards used for divination. It appeared in Northern Italy in the fifteenth century based on a card game that came from Egypt. There are four suits like the common play deck which has hearts, diamonds, clubs and spades. The four suits in tarot differ depending on the deck, but the following are often used: wands, pentacles, swords and cups. Unlike the play deck, which only has one card without a suit, the joker, the tarot has 22 cards with no suits. These are termed the major arcana and are numbered 0–21. Major arcana archetypes can be helpful in working through emotional issues, generating both positive and negative characteristics hidden in the unconscious to be sensed, released and balanced.

People read the tarot by asking a question and then shuffling the deck, cutting and dealing the cards in one of many prescribed layouts. Each card represents certain energy and the placement of the card has a given meaning. For example, layouts often have a home position, and, for example, if a two of swords lands in that place it could be read in the following manner. The two stands for balance, and the suit of swords deals with the mind. This card in this position can be interpreted as meaning the person who is having the reading feels mentally balanced about home. Some may want to experiment with reading a whole deck. That's not the purpose of this book, but rather to use the major cards as psychological archetypes. But for the curious see Appendix 3 for pointers on reading tarot.

This chapter, however, is not about reading the tarot, it is about using the major arcana as archetypes to focus awareness for the quest to open the mind. Each one is a personification of a discernible set of characteristics, the very definition of an archetype. Since the cards are 500 years old, they have stood the test of time and can be used by seekers wanting to become wise. Take the quiz in Appendix 1. Then read about the archetype in this chapter and see if it is a fit. Empower yourself to be playful, by throwing a card away that doesn't fit and intuitively finding another. Major arcana archetypes have both positive and negative characteristics, just like humans. For example, a person may be angry, which is seen as negative, and the person may also be generous. But each characteristic has its place. A person who gives too much may eventually get angry, which serves as a signal to step back and give less. Having both traits in awareness will help equilibrium, to use either characteristic as necessary. Choosing a tarot archetype can help a person bring all of their characteristics into awareness.

#0 FOOL

Innocence

This is the first card of the major arcana. It is the only holdover from the play deck. This archetype signifies innocence and beginnings. The fool is playful and intuitive, not wasting time worrying. The negative aspect of this archetype is being impulsive or reckless.

Figure 6.1 The Fool #0 is playful and open

Figure 6.2 Playful gymnastics personify the spontaneity of the Fool #0

Figure 6.3 The Fool #0 is similar to the jester, full of tricks and surprises

#1 MAGICIAN

Intuition

The magician is intuitive and can create rituals, waving a wand to materialize wishes. Organization and communication skills are natural to the magician. He works in the invisible realm to change the perceived world. There is no malice with the magician. He is powerful and knows he must set aside his own desires to effect change.

Figure 6.4 The Magician #1 has many tools to use to focus his intuition

Figure 6.5 With skill, the Magician #1 diverts attention to work his tricks

#2 HIGH PRIESTESS

Wisdom

The high priestess is sophisticated in her feminine spirituality. Connected to the Earth, she has keen insight and cuts to the heart of a matter. She can pull on the wisdom of the Earth to inform her actions, and represents knowledge and scholarship.

Figure 6.6 The High Priestess #2 has great power from her connection to the Earth

#3 EMPRESS

Abundance

The empress holds feminine power and rules through nurturance and knowledge of creation. She represents fertility, abundance, material wealth, domestic stability and prosperity. The negative side of this archetype can lead to financial difficulties.

Figure 6.7 The Empress #3 has many resources. She looks silly in this tarot card, but this belies her power

Figure 6.8 Mary is often seen as an Empress #3 since she symbolizes the connection of heaven to earth

#4 EMPEROR

Authority

The emperor represents control and power, and is the strongest male archetype of the major arcana. It deals with all things official in society, particularly in government and corporations, contracts, legality and money. This archetype can manage material affairs and can signify success in business. He is a strong leader and a faithful companion. The negative side is someone who is too authoritarian.

Figure 6.9 The Emperor #4 has gained authority through valor

Figure 6.10 Power can leave the Emperor #3 lonely, brittle and paranoid

Figure 6.11 An Emperor #3 can bring great good to his people,
but if he holds on to authority for too long disaster may be in his future

#5 HIEROPHANT

Spirituality

The hierophant is the spiritual teacher of the major arcana. He or she can bless others and respond to problems with wisdom. This archetype can give sage advice, and acts as a bridge between humanity and spirit. He is often looked at by society as a moral person. His negative side is harsh judgment.

Figure 6.12 The Hierophant #5 graces others with inspiring teachings

Figure 6.13 Sometimes the Hierophant #5 becomes too enmeshed in the superiority of his knowledge

Figure 6.14 Seeing spiritual truths, the Hierophant #5 may not conform to society's norms

#6 LOVERS

Union

The lovers represent joy with relationships, emotions and passions. This archetype represents being united with one's desires more than anything. It could be romantic love with another or uniting the opposites within oneself. It can signify the formation of true partnerships. The downside of this is using love as an escape from one's own issues.

Figure 6.15 The Lovers #6 signifies the joy from the union of opposites. It can be two people or two parts of the self, or something desired

Figure 6.16 With strong emotions sometimes comes delusion, and the Lovers #6 will take care to stay with authentic feelings in the heart

#7 CHARIOT

Success

The chariot represents making things happen in the physical world. He can triumph over obstacles, realize plans and experience success. This archetype has great will power to complete work. The negative side is pushing one's desires regardless of the context.

Figure 6.17 The Chariot #7 is capable of making difficult things happen and realizing plans

Figure 6.18 Single-minded focus and stamina are the Chariot's #7 strengths

#8 JUSTICE

Balance

Justice restores balance and rights wrongs. This archetype signifies the settlement of legal matters and contracts. Old scores are settled, and karma is achieved. Actions receive their logical reaction. This can either be positive or negative depending on what has come before.

Figure 6.19 Justice #8 balances wrongs of the past to create a level playing field

Figure 6.20 The blind figure of Justice #8
symbolizes the need for objectivity in being fair

#9 HERMIT

Solitude

This archetype is about being alone. It is a time to find inner peace. The alone period could prompt a time for prudence and planning. The downside can be loneliness.

Figure 6.21 The Hermit #9 chooses to be alone to tap inner resources for wisdom

Figure 6.22 Sometimes the Hermit #9
must retreat for protection

#10 WHEEL OF FORTUNE

Luck

This archetype has good luck. Chance will run its course and good things will happen. It is the end of a cycle and good fortune awaits. The possible negativity is not trusting in good luck.

Figure 6.23 The Wheel of Fortune #10 has lady luck at his or her side

Figure 6.24 The Wheel of Fortune #10 is open to possibilities, as the wheel spins

Figure 6.25 The Wheel of Fortune #10 brings optimism

#11 STRENGTH

Prowess

This is a wonderful archetype which represents physical, emotional and spiritual fortitude. One has the resources to accomplish goals and overcome obstacles. The negative side is self-indulgence and a loss of energy.

Figure 6.26 Strength #11 has many resources

Figure 6.27 The power of Strength #11 comes from building ties to others

#12 HANGED MAN

Surrender

This archetype is hanged by his heel as he lets go of universal energies. He has let go of all expectation and greets the future with open arms. He can adapt, sacrifice or change for a better future. This archetype contains the characteristic of surrender, and its negative side is resisting change.

Figure 6.28 The Hanged Man #12 personifies the paradox of letting go to find fulfillment

Figure 6.29 Grace and suppleness accompany the Hanged Man #12's release to natural forces

#13 DEATH

Loss

This archetype personifies the dramatic end of something and the beginning of a new cycle. It could be an abrupt change such as the loss of a job or a relationship, or it could be something more subtle like the realization that one has been blind to something. The Death archetype usually signifies a time of sadness. However, it could be a blessing in disguise. The negative aspect could be that a person is closed to the positive aspect of change.

Figure 6.30 Death #13 represents the end of old ways

Figure 6.31 Out of Death #13 something new is born, just as after a volcano erupts the rich soil spawns new life

#14 TEMPERANCE

Moderation

This archetype lives according to the Tao, finding a moderate way through problems as well as happiness. This individual has good management skills, can elicit cooperation, and can blend and synthesize opposites. It signifies a person who can create a space of peace, harmony and calm. The downside could be striving too hard for balance when a person is off kilter.

Figure 6.32 Temperance #14 is often depicted as a woman pouring water between two cups, showing that she must be fluid to exemplify moderation

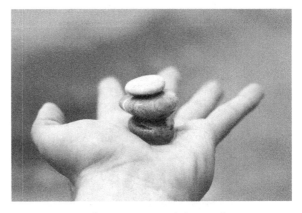

Figure 6.33 Balance is an essential element of Temperance #14, a quality that requires discipline and focus

#15 DEVIL

Delusion

This archetype lives in delusion. He has ideas or thinks things will happen that have no basis in reality and may have desires for physical and material things that are tied to people who are not trustworthy. The negative side is being attached to etheric notions and not being open to reality.

Figure 6.34 The Devil #15 represents delusion. He thinks he is powerful and can get everything he wants in life, but he can't

Figure 6.35 There is disappointment with the Devil #15's fantasy, but a release of expectations soothes the transition to reality

Figure 6.36 Humor helps the Devil #15 not take himself too seriously

#16 TOWER

Disruption

This archetype represents the breaking-up of structures. Change upends the cornerstone that has been the foundation of one's life. It could be through a conflict, or other difficulty. The downside is not embracing the change.

Figure 6.37 The Tower #16 signifies a sudden change

Figure 6.38 The Tower #16 also holds exciting possibilities of things to come

#17 STAR

Healing

This archetype personifies self-healing. The person has hope, confidence, vigor and can inspire others.

Figure 6.39 The Star #17 has the capacity to heal and renew

Figure 6.40 Self-healing depicts the Star #17

#18 MOON

Unconscious

This archetype is mysterious. Things are moving and shifting in the personal or collective unconscious. One can feel them but not put words on them. Intuitive sensations give previews of coming changes, sometimes in dreams or psychic visions. The negative aspect is being lost in dreams.

Figure 6.41 The Moon #18 represents changes afoot in the unconscious
only available through intuitive modes of expression such as dreams, poetry or art

Figure 6.42 With the Moon #18 things are not clear at first but clarity emerges

#19 SUN

Happiness

This archetype feels that everything is good. There is happiness, particularly with material resources such as money. He engenders good feelings that others can catch. There is abundance and achievement through success at work. The down side is holding on to the good times too long, resisting the new coming phase.

Figure 6.43 With the Sun #19, everything is quite all right

Figure 6.44 Everyone is happy with the Sun #19 shining

Figure 6.45 When the Sun #19 is shining one is in balance and harmony

#20 JUDGMENT

Renewal

This archetype represents the dawning of a new day. A certain set of circumstances have come to end. There is renewal and change for the better. The slate is clear and a new beginning is embraced.

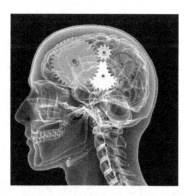

Figure 6.46 Judgment #20 signifies the creation of a new form

#21 WORLD

Fulfillment

This is the final archetype of the major arcana and signifies the integration of the spiritual and material world. This person can create a position of strength and culminate a task or period of life. The world is at her feet for travel, fun and pleasure.

Figure 6.47 The World #21 is the last card of the entire deck and is the card of wisdom and fulfillment. Spirit and matter are integrated

Figure 6.48 All life is sustained with the World #21

Figure 6.49 The World #21 becomes a symbol of humans' search for wisdom

CASE STUDIES

The following case studies show how people can work with a tarot archetype. These people could have found their archetype in several ways. First they could have taken the archetype quiz in Appendix 1. Or they could have pulled the 22 major arcana from a tarot deck, shuffled these cards, and then picked one at random.

Or they could have laid out all 22 cards face up, examining each, and chosen one that struck their fancy. Regardless of the method, these people selected a major arcana tarot archetype and began an encounter with the purpose of opening the mind to wisdom. The following stories show their interactions on their journeys.

■ TIMOTHY JUSTICE

Timothy had a hard life. He was bright but he never seemed to know how to talk to others. Social skills were out of his grasp, even though he was a true and loyal friend. He would do anything for someone he cared about. His closest mate, Charles, was a constant companion, but there came a time when this friend dumped Timothy, leaving him confused, sad and unhinged. The pattern of being rejected just seemed to follow Timothy—a friend would come but then go. No one stuck. Timothy developed a complex that people didn't like him. There was an undercurrent of sadness about him which made him reticent. He did make an effort, but always with the cloud of potential failure over him. He acted like he was fated to be unhappy, like the man who was born on Friday the 13th, 1913, who would never get on an airplane because his ill fortune would cause the plane to crash. Timothy didn't have a job and lived in a small room in a poor neighborhood in downtown Denver, supported by family money. One day he woke up and decided something had to change, and he returned to college to get a teaching degree.

Before he was to begin his first classes, he selected to draw a major arcana archetype card for advice. He drew the #8 Justice card. Timothy knew that the card represented righting the wrongs of the past. He decided to try to embody this archetype, to become Justice Timothy. To him, this card was about getting the karma deserved. He knew that it meant that for every action there was a reaction. He had been consistently kind and loyal to the people in his life. What would his karma be after these years of rejection? Surely the logical reaction to his actions would be a good turn of luck and acceptance. This would right the wrongs. In a self-analysis he wondered what it would take to embody justice. He decided he had to believe that his karma could balance his history of rejection with a future of acceptance. Timothy knew he would have to change his attitude that he would have bad luck, the negative self-view that seeped out in the way he acted in everyday life. A light came on, and he realized he needed to let go of the past. To move on, he had to open a space for the new.

Righting wrongs often happens with a legal system, and so the justice archetype refers to contracts and decrees. Timothy was going to go full board in embodying this card. He had worked hard and paid his dues, he was going for a scholarship. The legal forces would shine on him.

A surge of hope filled him, and he decided to study the picture on the card. The figure could have been a woman or man. It was androgynous. There was a sword in each hand pointing up to the sky. To him, the swords symbolized power to enforce decisions needed to right wrongs. Timothy knew he had to find the power in himself to make a change. Also signifying action, the swords implied that he had to do something about his situation. He had to take strong action to balance the playing field. He was in the right, and he would be validated by karma moving in a positive direction. He was ready for a better story and a new beginning.

ANNIE TEMPERANCE

Annie drew the #14 Temperance card, the archetype of moderation. Annie, a widow, had a very intense family situation. Her brother, Joseph, whom she was close to, had cancer. To help out she traveled from her home in Philadelphia to his home in Florida almost every month. She had two children and both had been out of the house for a while. But one, Alice, had just lost her job and was clinically depressed with no insurance or source of income. She returned to live with Annie, and because of her depression Alice was not a happy camper. As a result, day-to-day interactions were difficult. It was not hard for Annie to pay the bills since she had supported herself and her children for a long time, but the pressure was mounting. Almost at an early retirement age, she knew there would be no relief from financial pressure in the near future.

She had always been a fun-loving girl, ready to party, and often used this as an escape. But she was feeling the physical effects of alcohol abuse. Usually her optimistic temperament and work ethic kept her going. However, there was a deep sadness lurking near her waking moments, and deep fatigue reared its head often.

She realized she needed some help, and thought she'd give tarot a shot. After she drew the Temperance card, she sat and looked at the figure. In this deck, the card showed a woman with wings, pouring water from a cup to a bowl. The woman was standing on the shore of a large body of water. Annie put the card on her desk and studied it throughout her work day. Once in a while she would become quiet to look at the card, opening to the significance without prejudgment. She noticed that one foot was on the earth, and the other foot's toes were stuck in the water.

"Hmmmm," she thought, "maybe I need to put my toes in some water figuratively. Try something new."

The colors of the card were blue and yellow, which gave her a calm feeling. She thought she needed to remove herself from the hustle and bustle of daily life. Possibly it was not so difficult to find moderation in life. Maybe she could take a step back from her frantic life, calm herself and try to find some new ways. Looking again at the card, she noticed that the figure had wings. To Annie this represented the power to move and see things from a bird's eye view. If she had these skills she believed that she could find moderation within herself.

She thought about the stressors in her life stemming from all her financial responsibility. It felt like there was a large weight across her shoulders. She had grown used to it and in a strange way it seemed to give her stability. But it was too heavy now and it immobilized her. She needed to be free, and in the past partying was her way out, since she could be a wild girl and release that pressure. But this didn't work anymore, and she had grief at the loss of the relationship with her depressed daughter.

She wondered how she could use temperance to help her moderate between stress and partying. How could the moderation archetype help her from feeling trapped and sad, and transform this to liberation and happiness? First she thought, "I can become someone with equilibrium. I can remove myself from the daily stress and instead watch what is happening to me. I can find balance in my perception of my situation. I want to be still for a while and imagine I am pouring water, while I put my toes in the sea. If I can find that fluidity in myself, I can see what to do."

▌SALLY HIEROPHANT

Sally was in her mid-twenties and worked as a project officer for the Gill Foundation in Colorado Springs, Colorado, which was founded by Tom Gill, creator of the extremely successful graphics software, Quark. His foundation had a Gay and Lesbian Fund to help non-profits improve their fund-raising ability. Sally loved her work. She would be in downtown Denver at the Boys and Girls Clubs watching mentors inspire youth. She could take I-70 to Vail, and see paraplegics learn to ski. With a degree from Colorado University (CU) Boulder in social work, Sally was thrilled that she could walk her talk with her job. She was tall and thin, with auburn hair, dressing stylishly with Banana Republic or vintage thrift store items. As a Phi Beta Kappa in college, she was ready to succeed in the world of non-profits. Sally was consumed and passionate about helping others, and there was nothing she loved more than getting in debates with her friends about gay rights. But there was a problem. Her friends seemed to respect her, and invite her out to dinner once in a while, but often they would act cold or distant to her after she stood up for gay marriage or immigrants' rights. It was puzzling to her. She would listen to their ideas, so she wondered why they wouldn't listen to hers.

She was upset one night and wanted some guidance, so she pulled out the 22 major arcana from a tarot deck and shuffled. Sally drew the #5 Hierophant card, which engendered mixed feelings. It was a male, and he seemed old and ugly wearing robes and a crown. But as she read about the card she learned that the hierophant was a spiritual teacher. Sally could identify with this because she often felt she thought her life was about justice standing up for what was right. Frequently, she felt wiser than her years. She looked carefully at the card and noticed that the figure had one eye open while the other was shut. Nestled in the pocket of the archetype's robe was a doll with a two-tone face, white on one side and black on the other. The card evoked the concept of "opposites" to her. She wondered, "Do spiritual teachers know about opposites?" If hierophants were spiritual then they must be about opposites, which seemed confusing. Suddenly, she knew. The opposite of compassion was judgment. This made her think about how she presented her own views. Her views often had a moral tone. Standing up for the good at times might be perceived as judging others.

Being a spiritual teacher had to be about love, which was about accepting others, but the opposite of this was judging. A light turned on for Sally. She would embody the hierophant by being true to what she knew. But instead of trying, maybe she should try the opposite, she should try to relax. Leading by example was the ticket. She would give herself a break, resting in the knowledge she knew what was right, instead of speaking up about it all the time. She was empowered by the idea of trusting herself, but it was also a caution to be careful about judging others. It was a little scary to think of herself as a spiritual teacher, but she thought everyone had something to share, and she wanted people to be a force for good. She thought she would sit with the idea about living in compassion for a while, instead of worrying about who agreed with her ideas.

KRISTEN LOVERS

Kristen was a professor in history at an alternative university in Sebastopol, California. She was a hard worker and wanted to go far. However, Kristen's life was different than most of the people she encountered, since she had been diagnosed with bipolar disorder. This happened when she was in high school after a suicide attempt. It had been a tough road, getting back to school, going to a psychiatrist, experimenting with medication, finding friends who would accept her. But she had done it, building a life with the extra help of yoga, and imagery for relaxation. She had come far, but it was difficult.

Over the holidays she had had a party and invited everyone in her department. Louise, one of her snippy colleagues who was jealous of Kristen's publications, became nosey and went through Kristen's medicine cabinets. She found bipolar medication which she recognized since her sister had the disease as well. At the next faculty meeting during a particularly heated discussion when Kristen and Louise were on different sides, Louise said, "At least I'm not crazy." Kristen was furious and didn't know how to handle the situation. She didn't want to get in an open fight with her colleague, but she didn't want to let it go and be bullied again.

Turning to the major arcana for guidance, Kristen drew the #6 Lovers card. Her first response was a bit erotic. It showed a man and woman in a sexual embrace, but she knew the archetype wasn't only about sex between partners, but about the bigger concept of union. Union was the main word for this card, and it was about joy in being united with one's opposite. She had studied Carl Jung a bit, so she knew that symbolism in dreams, for example, was not necessarily about different people, but every character was some aspect of the dreamer. With this in mind, she wondered about what two parts of herself she could unite, not to strive to be better, but to find joy and to have fun.

She carefully examined the card, noticing the man and woman in embrace. The man was black and the woman ivory. A snake was at the foot of the man, and they were standing on the shore of a lake with mountains behind. A full moon was above, but there was a glow as dusk was fading. Mulling over the symbolism, she was struck by the scene, which included mountains, a lake and the moon. It seemed like a beautiful place to visit. Kristen realized how hard she worked and how little fun she had in life. She had a three-day weekend coming up, and decided to go to the beach, and forget about her mean-spirited colleague. She needed to unify with the part of her that could relax.

JOE DEATH

Joe was a Vice President in an investment bank in downtown Seattle. He had a happy life with a wife and two kids. Even though he wore Calvin Klein suits when he walked across from his high-rise office for lunch at Pike's Place, he prided himself as being a rebel. During the weekends, he wore skater shorts, and on winter days he took his board to neighborhood swimming pools for practice. As a rock-and-roll aficionado, he combed the Pacific Coast for the best music venues. Life was good. Maybe he was a little too much of a workaholic, maybe he boasted a little about his success coming from a working class family, but still all was copesetic. He had weathered the recession and was looking forward to a family vacation in the San Juan Islands in a month. But sometimes life creeps up on one. He was called into his boss's office and was told he was going to lose his job.

He needed help and looked to the tarot for guidance. Pulling a card that night, he was not surprised to get the #13 Death card. He had heard one of his friends who was an expert at tarot tell a story about this very card. Dahlia, that was her name, and the story came from when she was on the way to teach in India. She was waiting in the international lounge in Tokyo for her connection to New Delhi, doing a little tarot to pass the time and look into the future. She did several tarot layouts and each time the outcome card was Death, which was not the outcome she was looking for. Many people say there are no bad cards in tarot, but from experience she knew that if one got this card it wouldn't feel good. It turned out to be prescience, since Joe's friend had great difficulty in India. She was very ill, her boss was demeaning and demanding. Plus it was difficult to get food in the remote village in Gujarat where she lived. So when Joe pulled this card he knew there was difficulty ahead.

He wondered how he could embody this archetype. Halloween was far away, so he could dress as the Grim Reaper. This silly thought faded, and he became serious to think about what the death card meant. He knew it signified the end of something, but also the beginning of a cycle of rebirth. It seemed pretty straightforward, one of the basic human experiences, death and birth. Joe thought that even though U.S. society denies death while embracing birth, he needed to embrace this impending destruction. He decided to be with the sadness. Not knowing how long he needed to do this, he also had faith that this cycle would end and rebirth would come. He knew it might be long, so he would reach out for help to get through it. He was going to keep the cards on his home desk as a reminder, keeping the faith alive that out of death comes new birth. He made a decision to stay with the sadness of the current situation, to take care of himself physically, emotionally and spiritually and be ready for the opening that would come. This gave him peace.

CHAPTER 7

DEITY ARCHETYPES FOR SPIRITUAL AWARENESS

Deity archetypes are helpful when people want to develop spiritual awareness towards wisdom. This chapter presents five deity archetypes: Lilith, a middle Eastern goddess; Isis, the Egyptian empress; Gaia, the Greek Earth goddess; Ganesha, the elephant Hindu god; and Avalokiteshvara, the Buddha of compassion. Some are central to religions, but for purposes of transforming the mind to spaciousness these deities are psychological tools with the added benefit of embodying spiritual qualities. The survey in Appendix 2 will help the reader select an archetype as a starter.

LILITH

BRAVE, self-reliant, magical, sexual, independent

Figure 7.1 Original painting of Lilith by Ted Garcia
The wings denote the ability to transform and her reptilian
feet show her ancient connection to the Earth.

Origin

Lilith's name initially appears as a Mesopotamian goddess around 4200 BCE. A controversial figure, some sources describe her as a spirit who entraps men with seduction. However, others see her as an empowered feminine deity who is not subservient to God or Adam but who brings knowledge as liberation not evil. She is associated with Malkuth, which is one of the attributes of God in the Kabbalah tree of life, representing the divine in the physical dimension (Godwin 1990). She appears in Goethe's *Faust*, wrapping her hair around men and never letting go. There is a contemporary Australian journal on feminist history, named *Lilith*.

Story

In *The Alphabet of Ben Sira*, from the eighth to the tenth century BCE, she is said to be Adam's first wife, who was made out of dirt just as he was. Lilith did not like being underneath Adam consistently in the sex act and was thrown out of Eden. She came back as the serpent to tempt Eve with the apple from the Tree of Knowledge.

Symbolism

She stands for sexuality as well as knowledge. Her skills are flying and also standing up for herself when treated unfairly. She has transformational ability since she can change forms. Her test was whether or not she would be subservient to male authority. Her transformation was to find strength and return to Eden.

Interpretation

I was struck by Lilith, since her story had been suppressed. I had no idea that Adam had a wife before Eve. Also I was amazed that Lilith was such an amalgam of characteristics. She had claws like a reptile and wings like a bird, but yet she was a woman. She seemed to represent the Earth's animalistic strength and power. Yet she was venerable, wanting to be loved and accepted. Through her ostracism from Eden, she found knowledge and wisdom. She taught me that there are no mental models about how to be in the world. I had to find who I was through my experience, not through what I knew. As Adam's first wife, she discovered a path to express her voice about domination; even though she was rejected, she created a unique way to express her individuality.

Lilith's lesson: Accept oneself

Figure 7.2 As an eagle is brave, so is Lilith

ISIS

GENERATIVE, indestructible, immutable, powerful, magical, wise

Figure 7.3 Isis mated with her husband Osiris after he died and then birthed a great leader, Horus. She has the power to generate life

Origin

Isis is an Egyptian goddess appearing as early as 2500 BCE and is well known as the symbol of motherhood and simplicity. She is synonymous with the Nile, the bringer of life in the desert. Like the Nile's predictable floods she is an immutable symbol of the eternal cyclic ebb and flow of life. Her energy balances the opposites since, after the drought, floods return. Mentioned in the Book of the Dead, Isis is known for standing up for the poor and the weak. There is a scientific journal named after her, the *Isis Journal* (University of Chicago Press). It publishes articles on history of science, medicine, technology and their cultural influences (Baring and Cashford 1993; Olson 1994).

Story

Isis wanted to gain knowledge of the secret name of the Sun god, who held the mystery of creation. When he grew old, his mouth trembled and his spit fell to the ground during his morning walks across the sky. Stealthily Isis picked up the spit and made a snake out of it. She put it on his path the next morning. The snake bit him, and he screamed in pain. Isis said she would cure him if he told her his real name. He tried to trick her with false names, but she was not fooled. He finally told her the unknowable name, Re, which she could then use to create life.

Isis was married to Osiris. Both were from a set of quadruplets, and Seth, their brother, was jealous. He killed Osiris and hid the body, since he knew Isis might be able to raise him from the dead with Re's power. After learning of the murder, Isis and her sister Nephthys searched unceasingly for his body by winging over the desert. Finally, they found it on a sand bank in the Nile. He was dead, but Isis mated with him anyway and birthed Horus. The boy became a great ruler of Egypt, predating the story of the immaculate conception of Jesus.

Symbolism

Isis stands for earth and fertility and has other wonderful characteristics. She is smart and can use trickery to find the truth. She fooled the Sun god Re to give her his secret. She could fly just like Lilith and was able to find her dead mate. Her test was moving on after her mate was killed, and her transformation was enduring amidst tragedy. Most importantly, she could create life from her own body. She was self-sustaining and generating just like Sophia the Gnostic Creator.

Interpretation

I really like that Isis was able to trick Re out of the knowledge of his real name, which gave her his power. She figured out a strategy to gain potency and used this to do good things such as ruling Egypt beneficently and creating an heir. She also had great perseverance and would not give up until she found the body of her husband. Further, she had the ability to transform, as demonstrated by her ability to grow wings and fly. Power, perseverance and transformation are important qualities on the spiritual path.

Isis's lesson: Have confidence and take action

Figure 7.4 Choosing Isis as an archetype helps foster creative energy

Figure 7.5 Isis represents beauty in her creative abilities

GAIA

PROTECTIVE, earthly, creative, sustaining,
magical, wise, everlasting, available

Figure 7.6 Gaia protects all life on the Earth, as one living organism

Origin

She is the ancient Greek goddess of the Earth. Her name is derived from the root words for Earth and Grandmother. She represents fertility and the primordial creative forces of the Earth.

Story

Gaia created the sea, mountains and sky. With her mate, Ouranos, she co-parented the twelve Titans and the one-eyed Cyclops. Her mate thought the Cylops were ugly and wanted to destroy them. To protect them, she hid them in her depths. However, she was afraid of Ouranos and thought he might obliterate others of their children. She enlisted the help of their son, Cronos. The next time Ouranos came to make love, she asked Cronos to cut off his father's genitals, which he did, and then threw them in the ocean. The blood from his wound gave birth to the giants and nymphs, and when the genitals were thrown into the sea Aphrodite was created. Ouranos was then banished to the sky. Later Cronos wanted to take the place of his father, and it was predicted that one of Cronos' children would defeat him. Following in his father's footsteps he tried to kill his children. Gaia could not stand to see her grandchild killed so she tricked Cronos in swallowing a stone instead of Zeus, laying the groundwork for him to become the most important god and defeat her own son (Baring and Cashford 1993; Olson 1994).

Symbolism

Her test was to stand up to authority to sustain life even though she defied her husband and son. She found great inner strength to do this. Her story is reminiscent of Ganesha's. He protected his mother from Shiva, just as Gaia did for the Cyclops. They preserved life. Gaia is also similar to Isis and Lilith in refusing to be dominated. They all stood up for what they thought was correct.

Interpretation

It is hard not to be in awe of the sheer magnitude of Gaia. After all, she represents the totality of the Earth and its many life forms. Gaia never failed to protect life, even standing up to her mate, to make sure the deformed Cyclops were not destroyed. Scientists have appropriated Gaia's name for the concept that the Earth is one living breathing organism, from the krill in the oceans to the ten-thousand-year-old bristlecone pines in the mountains. Humans are a part of this vast strength, since they are made out of the same medium.

Gaia's lesson: Protect life

Figure 7.7 Choosing Gaia as an archetype helps one feel the joy of being alive

GANESHA
GENEROUS, helpful, loving, kind, earthly

Figure 7.8 Ganesha suffered greatly when his head was cut off, but his sacrifice gave him great gifts to share with others. He represents beneficence at new beginnings, particularly with the possibilities of riches in the new endeavor

Origin

Ganesha is a Hindu god, first emerging in the fourth and fifth centuries CE in the scriptures called Ganesha Purana, the Mudgala Purana and the Ganapati Atharvashirsa (Grimes 1995).

Story

I reviewed Ganesha's story earlier, as a metaphor for disabling the ego's control of the mind. Briefly, Ganesha's mother Parvati asked him to guard her from his father's affection while she was bathing. Shiva, the Hindu god of destruction and his father, was furious, and cut off his head. After his mother's pleading, he had a servant bring the nearest head, which was an elephant's. A deity of new beginnings and riches was created.

Symbolism

Ganesha's mother, Parvati, represents nature, change and potency whereas his father, Shiva, represents transcendence, immutability and latency. Ganesha is a divine child brought to birth from dirt. He removes obstacles, creates new beginnings and possesses many *siddhis*, which are psychic gifts stemming from spiritual wisdom. In Hindu philosophy, Ganesha is said to symbolize the base chakra of the seven energy centers. The base chakra is about a person's physicality, showing that Ganesha connects spirit to matter. He can remove the obstacle of ignorance, since realization opens the threshold from the material world to spirit.

Interpretation

His test was how to change the pain of being dismembered to becoming a magnificent half-animal and half-human god. His transformation was to integrate animal and human energy into spirituality. He was of the Earth, but also of spirit, gracing all those he met.

Ganesha was made out of clay, like Lilith. Both archetypes teach the integral connection between the material and spirit world. Ganesha opens the door to finding spirit in the human condition.

Ganesha's lesson: Relax the ego

Figure 7.9 With his great strength Ganesha can remove obstacles

Figure 7.10 Ganesha represents the beauty of letting go of one's control of reality

AVALOKITESHVARA

COMPASSIONATE, helpful, graceful, eternal, giving, loving

Figure 7.11 Avalokiteshvara

Avalokiteshvara was enlightened and as a bodhisattva had sworn not
to be saved until all were saved. He was so overcome with his task of relieving
human suffering, that his head broke into many pieces. The Buddha gave him
10,000 arms and ten heads to show him that he had many resources for his work.

Origin

His story was first written in the Kanjur, the Tibetan Buddhist
canons from the fourth century CE. Avalokiteshvara stands for
infinite compassion. His other names are Chenrezig in Tibet, and
Kwan Lin, a woman goddess in China. The current Dalai Lama is
said to be an incarnation of Chenrezig (Loori 2008).

Story

He lived in a pure land, and saw through his clairvoyance how sentient beings were gradually becoming enlightened. As I've described in an earlier chapter, he was filled with anguish when he realized that no matter how many transcended, there would still be many more who did not. There was no way he could help them all, and the emotions that took him over cracked his head into a hundred pieces. Amitabha, a form of the Buddha, who was in the pure land with him, said, "Don't worry. You can still help free all beings from suffering." He blessed the pieces of Avalokiteshvara and gave him ten heads and ten thousand arms, as well as a thousand eyes to see what needed to be done.

Symbolism

His motto was, no one gets there unless we all get there. He had taken the bodhisattva pledge to not enter Nirvana until all sentient beings could. His test was to face the enormity of the task and deny himself peace. His transformation was to become pure compassion and make it available in an unending manner. The symbolism was to have his head broken into many pieces, and then have it be reformed into ten heads and ten thousand arms to help others. This means that when one gives up trying to do things on one's own, then help rushes in. The mind can be transformed to spaciousness. Then the ego's delusion of individuality and control can be relaxed. Spirit then rushes in with the forces that Gaia and Isis had harnessed.

Interpretation

Avalokiteshvara literally falls apart when he is faced with the enormity of human suffering. He travels to a pure land and the Buddha gives him the gifts of many heads and arms. Just as Ganesha found gifts after severe injury, this archetype did as well. Transformation can be painful, but the result is a joyous state full of compassion with a direct link to the spiritual world.

Avalokiteshvara's lesson: Trust the inner Self

*Figure 7.12 With attributes of both the feminine and the masculine,
Avalokiteshvara conveys wholeness*

*Figure 7.13 Standing for compassion, Avalokiteshvara
shows people how to have a gentle heart*

CASE STUDIES

Identifying with an archetype gives a focus, relaxing the ego and opening the mind. This doesn't happen overnight. It is not a quick fix, and it takes practice. Over time the inner world is transformed to the subtle state of being spiritual all the time. The new inner state is not necessarily accompanied by continual highs, control, good emotions, or the ability to manifest desires. Rather, the mind is transformed so that it is wise, soft, friendly, warm and spacious. The following case studies show how people have used the deity archetypes to accomplish this.

I have tried these ideas out with a number of people for quite a few years, and have created these case studies to show how the process works.

■ SAMUEL AND LILITH

Samuel went to a workshop, took the archetype quiz and selected Lilith. At first he didn't like her. She was a woman, which he was not. His distaste faded when he remembered that all humans had both feminine and masculine dimensions, making him feel better.

But then he went back to a negative mindset, because he recalled that Lilith had an unsavory past. After all, she had claws on her feet and wings on her back, and she could transform into a serpent. His revulsion disappeared when Samuel remembered that an archetype is not a real person, but is mythical and represents a collection of characteristics, an invisible energy pattern. He recalled an example of this, thinking of a rainbow and the spectrum that happens when light passes through a prism. Light is energy that can be seen but is not tangible. It is invisible at first, but in the early morning as the Sun hits the prism, a rainbow shines on the opposite wall. Samuel remembered that he could see a pattern, red, orange, yellow, green, blue, indigo and violet. But when he put his finger out to touch it, there was nothing there. This was a good analogy to understand archetypes. After thinking about prisms, Samuel tried to see the pattern that Lilith represented, instead of thinking about describing her as if she was real. He thought, "No humans have claws, but maybe Lilith represents something I can use."

He started trying to see what he should be getting out of her story. For example, she was treated unfairly and thrown out of Eden. Samuel could relate: he often felt put down. But there are other parts of her story that he could not relate to. He disapproved of the fact that she came back as a serpent to tempt Eve, even though he questioned if eating the apple from the tree of life was a bad thing. Certainly, knowledge could be better than ignorance.

All these thoughts kept rolling around his mind, and he finally decided to do some more research about Lilith. He searched the Internet and found pictures to print and stories to read. He went to the bookstore and discovered books about Middle Eastern goddesses. After a while this all seemed too "touchy-feely." He quit, but found a postcard picture of Lilith which he put on his bulletin board.

During this search, he saw a picture of Hercules in one of the books about gods and goddesses, and decided that he liked him a lot better. Remembering the idea from the workshop that all archetypes contain every other one, he decided to switch. He got a new postcard of Hercules and put that beside Lilith on the bulletin board.

The characteristics that he liked about Lilith were that she was strong and unconquerable, but conciliatory when needed. She was also beautiful in a wild way, willing to take responsibility for her actions and endure negative consequences. What he liked about Hercules was that he was shiny, golden and brave. But he was vulnerable too, like Lilith. He found this an interesting commonality of both archetypes, since they were both strong but wounded. Hercules even asked for his own death at the end to relieve suffering.

Samuel thought that, just like the archetypes, he was vulnerable. He realized that he had never let himself connect with this quality. This realization helped him a lot. He now saw that he could be stronger if at certain times he could admit his fear and insecurity. After several months, Samuel lost interest in both archetypes, but if he thought about it, he realized that something had changed inside of him. He felt more whole, he had more capacity to get on with his daily life and was more resilient. There were ups and downs, but he seemed to bounce back faster.

THALIA AND AVALOKITESHVARA

Thalia was a graduate student in eighteenth-century English history. She loved the Victorian period when women dressed in stiff finery, and men were formal and respectful. At the same time, she knew from novels that repressed sexuality was rampant in Edward VII's day. It all seemed prim and proper, but at the same time people were screwing each other in the bathrooms at house parties. The fact that the polarities of salaciousness and proprietary co-existed fascinated her. At a workshop, she took the archetype quiz and found that her archetype was Avalokiteshvara. She was shocked, since she thought she would get Lilith, a sensual and sexual creature. But no, instead she got an archetype that represented the characteristics of the current Dalai Lama, the one that signified ultimate compassion from the heart.

Thalia had never thought of herself as compassionate. This quality depicted a person who was cool and cerebral and inhabited the etheric dimension of life. She didn't see herself that way. Rather, she was drawn to the visceral side of the human condition. The homeless on the street who smelled of wine and reached out with grasping hands for a few pennies, these were the ones that captured her attention, or the prostitutes she had seen on a visit to Geneva, Switzerland. Their bright red miniskirts and fishnet stockings reminded her to feel human. She had seen these women while with her 14-year-old daughter. She and her daughter had been walking to their hotel from the train station, and she had never thought that they would see prostitutes on the way. It was a shock, and she had wanted to jump in front of her daughter to block her view. Thalia and a prostitute exchanged glances, but both quickly looked away, embarrassed.

As this memory flooded Thalia's mind, she realized her interest in sexuality was voyeuristic. It wasn't real, but rather her way of rebelling in the world of academia. Maybe she would give Avalokiteshvara another chance. She was drawn to love humankind, generated from the heart. Visceral was the right word for her interest, but it was neither about prostitutes nor Edward VII. It was about love from the heart.

Thalia embraced Avalokiteshvara and decided to learn his story, reading it here, finding it on the Internet and discovering other versions in bookstores. She found out that this archetype was not removed and cerebral. He worked in villages with the poorest of the poor. She learned that compassion wasn't removed from the human experience.

By focusing on Avalokiteshvara, her unconscious was held open to release suppressed memories and emotion. All of a sudden she saw that she had overcome insecurity by shocking others with her sexually charged comments. Once she was aware of this, she realized she could let it go, relax, and not make a point of being different. Then she could naturally sense the heart of compassion. Her work with Avalokiteshvara helped her join the human race. She was more secure in herself and relaxed with others.

RANDALL AND GANESHA

Randall was a civil engineer. He had been a planner since he was an eight-year-old boy, sitting in a tree deciding that he would build roads and bridges one day. His careful life worked, as his calculated plans came to fruition in a perfect fashion. He had found the right girlfriend in college, Alice. She was malleable and thought that Randall was as close to perfection as the roadways he designed. He finished school with a 4.0, did a summer internship with the company he wanted to work for and landed a high-paying job at the end of the summer. The young couple bought a small, fixer-upper bungalow. After a few coats of paint and small renovations, Randall planned to sell and roll the equity into a better and bigger house. At the engineering firm, Randall was promoted to project manager of a major exchange renovation merging two interstates.

But one night, everything changed. On the way home from a friend's party, Alice's car hit black ice, did a 360 degree turn and slammed into the rail guard. Alice was no more. All of Randall's carefully laid plans exploded into six months of intense grief. Randall could not go to work, get out of bed or feed himself. He knew he would not be moving through Elizabeth Kubler Ross's grief stages of denial, anger, bargaining, depression and acceptance. He was going to stay with anger as long as possible. It wasn't right that Alice died. Particularly, since he had been a good man and followed the rules. No longer was he in charge of things. Life wasn't fair.

One morning he woke up and his heart hurt really badly. It felt like the jagged edges of a hole in the ice. The edges were ragged and sharp, revealing a feeling like ink-black, frigid water. Something changed, Randall had an epiphany. It finally dawned on him that he was not in control anymore, since his life was unfolding on its own now. Out of desperation, he went to a self-help workshop.

There he took an archetype quiz, and found Ganesha. At first he didn't like the idea of a Hindu god. Everything from India was outside of his comfort zone: incense, pungent smelly food, rickshaws, and men nearly naked except for a piece of fabric that seemed like a skirt. But he was distraught and needed help, so he decided to do a careful read of Ganesha's story. Surprisingly, he found that he liked the elephant man. In fact, he liked him a lot. Growing up as a prince, the young man had everything at his disposal including money, travel, servants and riches. But he wasn't turned by wealth, since he was a devoted son following his mother's wishes for protection. He was a rule-follower, just like Randall. Possibly it was naïve for Ganesha to come between his mom and Shiva, the god of destruction. For his good intentions, he was mortally wounded, just like Randall was after his wife's death. His life had taken a macabre and surprising turn. No one would have chosen this. No one would choose to get an elephant head. He surrendered, because everything was out of his control. Randall could relate since he too could no longer plan life. But he had found hope in this story because out of death, trauma and grief, good things flowed.

The engineer went to the closest Indian store and bought a little statue of Ganesha, putting it next to his favorite picture of Alice. Some nights he would light a votive candle, gold with a vanilla scent. Grief didn't go away, but his anger lessened. The sharp points of ice in his heart melted a little. He relaxed instead of trying to control his life.

◼ VERONICA AND ISIS

Veronica was a stockbroker living in Brooklyn, the new Manhattan. She was very pretty with straightened hair and long legs. She dressed the part with four-inch black heels and pin-striped designer suits with a fuchsia or turquoise silk shirt peeking out. The style was feminine but formal. Her life was on a high since she had a well-paid job at Goldman Sachs, a sequence of good-looking lovers and a cheery condo. But the good life crashed to a halt when she was laid off and only had savings for three mortgage payments. Things were serious, but she was committed not to go back to Carbondale, Illinois, with her tail between her legs. At her local coffee shop she noted a flyer for an archetype workshop. She attended and found Isis.

This did not go well for Veronica at first, since she equated Isis with the Afrocentric stores in downtown Carbondale. People who worked there wore dashikis with huge necklaces of brown wooden beads, sometimes with an ankh in the middle. She knew this was Isis' symbol. Veronica was proud of her African heritage but she wanted to join mainstream society, showing everyone that she was as good as they were.

Her first reaction was rejection. She didn't want to go back to her roots since she was just fine the way she was. She was always proud of her heritage, but she didn't need to work on it. She would do anything, though, to jump back into the job market to keep her upwardly mobile ascent, and she was not a person to give up. She'd give Isis a try.

She read Isis' story and bought a statue at a nearby New Age bookstore. At home, she found a special place for it near a window so that the ancient Egyptian ruler could look out at her garden. After she let go of her stereotype of disgust, she noticed some things about the archetype. What struck Veronica was Isis' strength, since she had done everything in her power to find her dead husband's body and never gave up. It also fascinated her that the goddess could find out the Sun god's name. This took remarkable fortitude and clarity of purpose.

Veronica decided that she had just as much strength and determination as Isis and could direct it to find a new job. Just as Isis used craft and strategy to find Re's name, she could do the same. Instead of being ashamed that she didn't have a job, she could call up old contacts at the trading house with confidence. The next time she went to an open-air art market, she bought two paintings from Kenya and a wooden bead necklace. Isis helped Veronica open up to the ties to her African heritage, giving her more reserves to draw on.

TED AND GAIA

Ted was a mountain climber who had conquered Mt. Hood and Mt. Whitney and acted as support to a group ascending K2 in the Hindu Kush. Raised by a loving mother and a distant father, he grew up in Missouri. He thought of himself as a well-adjusted and balanced person. Most people told him he had a positive feminine side, as well. Not sure of what this meant, he accepted it. After all, he had learned to knit socks, even though baking bread had eluded him. Sometimes he felt conflicted, confident in his masculinity, but confused by how people reacted to him. He was physically strong and aggressive when he needed to be, and he didn't take put-downs from anyone. If someone called him a pussy, he might want to hit the jerk, but usually he came up with a cryptic put-down such as, "Well, at least I am not an ignorant moron." He also thought of himself as full of heart. He could comfort his friend, Angie, when her dog died or he would pop bills into the Salvation Army's buckets at Christmas in front of Walgreens.

At the same time, he came up dumbfounded once in a while. Kerri, his girlfriend, told him he didn't support her emotionally. Last week, she had learned that she lost her teaching job. She was crying and upset. Ted sat down beside her, hugged her and said, "Let's figure this out. You're smart and you have options. We could move. Let me help. I could make copies of your résumé."

Kerri pulled away and looked at him aghast, narrowing her eyes and saying with exasperation, "I don't want you to solve my problem. I want you to be here for me. Have you ever heard of the word empathy?"

Empathy was an elusive concept to Ted. He did feel sad when he saw dolphins slaughtered or when he was at a train station in Chennai, India, looking at a man without legs. But he had no idea what Kerri was talking about. He thought, "How was this not empathy? I was helping her solve her problem."

Kerri continued her diatribe against him. "You need to be in your heart more. Find something to open your heart."

The next day Ted was at the bookstore, and he remembered Carl Jung's idea from his psychology classes. He recalled the idea of being whole, letting all that was inside open up, particularly those things hidden in the unconscious. He had thought he was already in his heart. After all, he listened, hugged and cooked, didn't he? But maybe he was missing something. According to Kerri, he had further to go.

All of a sudden in the bookstore, he had a vivid memory of an intuition exercise from the class. The teacher had put a lot of objects around the room. The students were to close their eyes, turn around 360 degrees and then use their body sense to walk to an object. Supposedly they could find something significant. According to that teacher, the kinesthetic sense never lied. In class, Ted had walked to a purple geode. He didn't know how meaningful it was, but he sure liked it. After all, he loved the Earth since he was a mountain climber. He never felt so alive as when he was on a mountain, holding on to a piece of granite.

Standing in a bookstore with a cup of fair trade, organic Guatemalan coffee in his hand, he put down the cup, walked to the spiritual book section, closed his eyes and did a complete turn. He put his hand out, running it across rows of books. All of a sudden his palm felt hot. Opening his eyes, he saw he was touching a book about Gaia, the Greek Earth goddess. It reminded him of the purple geode, and he opened it.

Since he had the afternoon off, he went back to get his coffee, settled into a comfortable, leather chair in a corner and read. Then he read some more. Gaia was feminine, but huge and strong. She was accommodating to her mate Ouranos up to a point, but she could be violent. Ted found much of her behavior bizarre and hard to relate to. He didn't like her deception in hiding stones instead of the Cyclops. But he also felt most people would do things that they wouldn't be proud of to accomplish goals. The main characteristic that drew his attention was that she was always aware and present. Nothing seemed to distract her. She was always there, watching, creating and protecting. It gave him some idea of what Kerri wanted from him.

In the next few weeks, Ted noticed his intuition was very active. He started going to a meditation group that he had visited the year before. He would spontaneously take a walk if he felt stressed and was about to lose it. Gaia seemed to have wrought subtle changes within him. He was not different, but at the same time, he had a little more space inside.

CHAPTER 8

ARCHETYPAL IMAGERY: PUTTING IT ALL TOGETHER

This chapter will put all the earlier concepts together to show coaching and therapy applications. Up to this point the book has covered a wide range of both theoretical and practical information including psychological and Vedantic models of the mind, brain physiology, imagery research and stories of archetypes. The practitioner may be wondering how to put all this into action. The purpose of this chapter is to present practical pointers for sessions. These are designed to empower clients to work with current emotional issues while softening the ego's hold on the unconscious to reach both emotional and spiritual goals. Even though the sessions are presented in a "how-to" cookbook fashion, it is assumed that the coach or therapist will trust his or her own process, experience, knowledge and intuition in guiding the process using what seems to fit. There are a number of activities in each session, and they can be broken out and distributed across sessions or cycled through as the practitioner deems appropriate. The chapter begins with some background on assumptions for working with emotions and imagery.

BACKGROUND

The sessions rely on humanistic psychology principles primarily based on the work of Carl Rogers (1961) and Fritz Perls (1992). Their model for emotional health posits a creative force in the unconscious that will lead a person to insight for positive change. This force is activated by a safe environment which allows emotions to be sensed and cleared. Rogers recommended a number of conditions to create safety, including non-judgment and authenticity on the part of the practitioner. Extending his ideas, it is recommended that practitioners create a safe space through acceptance and active listening. Fritz Perls, the founder of gestalt theory, was a bit more forceful than Rogers, confronting clients' incongruences between non-verbal and verbal behavior, for example. His main point applied here is to be aware of non-verbal behavior and to help clients focus on emotions in the body. One of his most important teachings was that an emotion needed to be accepted before it changed.

But both taught that emotional health came through sensing emotions so that they could be released, and that a creative force in the unconscious would lead a client to healing when given a chance. So in part, a practitioner's job is to get out of the way of a client's process, or at least create a safe container for it to work. The humanist psychologists also thought that the body was a direct link to the creative force. Because of this the directions for the sessions encourage clients to sense emotions in the body.

Overlapping humanistic psychology pointers are those from research on how to lead effective imagery (Nelson 1993). These guidelines used to vivify archetypal imagery will become a practitioner's best friend. One principle is that people's images have their own integrity, and it is best for the practitioner to stay with the client's image and work within the reality he or she is creating, as opposed to interpreting it. Images will carry their own meaning for the client, and they can be silly or have dark themes, but the idea is for the practitioner to help the client transform the images in a way that feels congruent towards a positive frame. Sometimes it is almost like creating a cartoon.

BASIC TECHNIQUES AND ASSUMPTIONS

1. Emotions can transform if they are sensed and then accepted.

2. It's best to keep the client from analyzing or going "cognitive." Asking clients to use present tense and focusing on perceptual details in memories or images helps this.

3. Keep yourself from trying to figure out the meaning of images or memories, but try to visualize those with the client, so that your body and intuitive sense are active.

4. Go with what emerges from the client's imagination. Magical or silly transformations are fine. Trust the client's deep Self in generating information that is needed. If you make suggestions for imagery or goals, check in with the client to see if they feel right. Encourage the client to use his or her body response as a check for authenticity.

SESSION 1

Step 1: Settle in

Before the first session, ask the client to purchase a sketch book and set of colored pencils. The purpose of this session is to orient the client to this book's Wise Mind–Body model which shows how relaxing the ego through archetypal imagery opens the unconscious for emotional release and spiritual insight. The second purpose is to choose a goal for the coaching sessions. It is best to begin the session with normal grounding and setting boundaries and/or norms for the work together.

Step 2: Motivate the client to participate in archetypal imagery

Explain the purposes of the first session. Then review the assumptions of the Wise Mind–Body model and the process of archetypal imagery below. If working face to face, or in a remote video format, Figure 1.8 from Chapter 1 could be used. You can use the summaries below or adapt them to the client's personal lens, as appropriate. This is a review of information from earlier chapters condensed in a form that might work for clients. The main idea is to give the client a model of transforming the mind to spaciousness by relaxing the ego, and motivate the work of opening the unconscious through archetypal imagery.

The Wise Mind–Body (see Figure 1.8, Chapter 1)
This coaching model assumes that humans have four bodies, the spiritual, physical, emotional, and mental which is usually controlled by the ego. The ego is a positive part of human psychology, giving stability, organizing the personality and establishing a sense of self. But over time it becomes rigid, skewing perceptions and relegating uncomfortable thoughts and sensations to the unconscious. This is accomplished by eating up mental energy, and restricting both rational and intuitive thinking and emotional awareness. However, if one softens the ego and thereby the barrier to the other bodies, this in effect creates a more spacious mind. Information from the other bodies, emotional, physical and spiritual, can enter conscious awareness.
Examples:

- The physical body holds emotional memories and using the kinesthetic sense to feel them may release them. If there is some trauma, for example of a negative interaction with a family member, it might be stored in the back of the neck as someone tenses up. This could have long-term physical consequences. Opening up to these sensations can release this tension. Also, the physical body is the primitive intuitive sense, as in a "gut feeling." Increased mental space allows a person to more easily sense these perceptions which sometimes are linked to safety, but also can give creative insights.

- The emotional body senses and reacts to the world around it. Usually these are markers of something that needs to be paid attention to and can be tied to past experiences. For example, if someone is very anxious that a close friend is not calling him or her back and it seems that it is an overreaction to a situation, then it could be tied to past difficult relationships. If the ego is rigid then this emotion may be outside of awareness, but cause a strong anxiety response. Softening the ego lets a person feel the emotion, bring awareness to it, and discharge its valence.

- The spiritual body is connected to the energetic domain where time and space connect in non-linear ways, creating enough mental space to allow insights, states of bliss and peace.

- Through archetypal imagery the mental/ego body can transform to awareness, holding a space to integrate rational and intuitive thought, emotions, memories and bodily sensations.

Archetypal imagery stages (see Figure 1.6, Chapter 1)

The ego likes paying attention to things. Giving it an archetype to image distracts the ego to soften the barrier to the unconscious mind and allow it to unfurl. As a reminder, an archetype is a discernible pattern of characteristics, such as a hero, a warrior, a teacher, a seducer. The unique quality of an archetype which makes it particularly useful for transformation is that it resides in the unconscious. As the ego pays attention to one it creates a natural connection to the unconscious mind, which will safely release material. Choosing an archetype consciously is a powerful tool to unify conscious intention with unconscious processing.

Figure 1.6 from Chapter 1 shows the transformation.

Step 3: Create a scenario

The next step is to help the client pinpoint a recent emotionally charged event to use as a basis for formulating a coaching goal. Ask him or her to think about a time in the last several weeks when something happened that they didn't like or didn't feel good about. To vivify the memory, encourage remembering as if it is actually happening, probing perceptual details of the event.

Some questions can assist this process. Location? Sequence of events? Who else was there? Colors? Clothes? Ask him or her to talk through the event in detail. Then ask for the location in the body where he or she feels something when remembering the scene. You may give some suggestions depending on what you are picking up, a knot in the stomach for example. But don't push too much. Keep working with the client until something comes up.

Then work with the client to come up with a goal or positive statement of how they want to deal with the feeling. Hopefully this would be a positive statement that will have some emotional content. Have the client write it down, and do so as well in your notes. Also note the disturbing scenario and the emotion that the client isolated. See the worksheet at the end of this chapter as a possible tool to keep track of key coaching elements.

Step 4: Archetype quiz, homework for next session

Ask the client if he or she sees the goal as emotional or spiritual, and then guide them to the appropriate archetype quiz (tarot for emotional and deity for spiritual goals; see Appendices 1 and 2). Give him or her directions to complete the homework assignment below for the next session.

Step 5: Archetype quiz, homework for next session

Direct your client to Appendix 1: Tarot Archetype Quiz, or Appendix 2: Deity Archetype Quiz. Tell the client to do the homework assignment below after choosing an archetype.

HOMEWORK: ARCHETYPE AMPLIFICATION ASSIGNMENT

Complete the (tarot or deity) archetype quiz. Use the key to select an archetype. If there is any confusion, for example if you have several archetypes, from the quiz then go with the one that you are attracted to. You can also work with more than one if you would like.

In your journal:

1. Write the name of your archetype.

2. After you read about the archetype, write the name in the journal, write any thoughts that come to mind, draw anything that comes to you with a colored pencil or pencils—maybe just swatches of color.

3. Possibly, if it feels right, find the archetype on the Internet, read, and afterwards write anything that comes to mind in your journal. Draw anything or just make splotches of colors with the colored pencils if it feels right. Print things from the Internet if it feels right. Cut pictures and paste in your journal. Be gentle with yourself and allow symbolism to emerge. Slowly, quietly with gentleness.

4. Possibly, if it feels right, go to a bookstore or library, and find information about the archetype. After you read, write in your journal anything that comes to you if it feels right.

SESSION 2

Step 1: Check in

Do a check-in of last week and what has been happening. Review the goal and see if it still feels right. Talk about anything that has emerged in the last week.

Step 2: Review archetype research

Ask the client to share any information or thoughts from the archetype quiz. If technologically possible, look at any drawings or notes from the archetype that he or she has found. Spend some time with this. The next step is to help the client come up with a characteristic of the archetype that stands out for him or her. You could make some suggestions. Then see if it is natural to talk about how the characteristic might have helped with the scenario. Let this discussion go where it feels right. It may be that it would be good to create another scenario, and do parts of Session 1 again, for example talking through another event in detail. Use your judgment about taking the next step of the archetype imagery.

Step 3: Archetypal imagery exercise

The next step is to do an archetypal imagery exercise. This is the touchstone of this coaching technique. Frequently, at this point the archetype selected by using the quiz may transform with the client's own imagination.

IMAGERY EXERCISE: ARCHETYPE

What follows is a lengthy relaxation sequence. Use your judgment about how much of the detail to use. In any case allow the client to settle in, take some breaths and relax before the specific imagery.

Take a moment to relax. Feel your whole body getting heavier and warmer. Uncross your legs and relax your hands. Close your eyes or keep them open. There are not rules in imagery, so just let you inner self unfold. Go to the right foot. Relax your big toe, second, third, fourth and the little toe. Relax your right calf, knee, go underneath your knee cap, and relax your quadriceps, the biggest muscle in the body. Relax your right hip. See the ball and socket. In your mind's eye open the socket slightly. Relax your left foot. Your left big toe, second, third, fourth and little toe. Relax your left calf, knee, underneath the knee cap, relax the left quadriceps. Visualize your left hip ball and socket. Open it slightly in your mind's eye. Relax your stomach, your heart. Think about your lungs, how they go down to your diaphragm in front, and low on your back by your floating ribs. See your rib cage move out slightly on either side by your arm on your next inhalation. Breathing is a passive activity, as you create space the air will rush in. Take another breath, see your ribs moving laterally towards your arms. Relax your heart. Give a firm, positive suggestion to your heart to slow down. Thank your heart gently for beating so many times a minute and keeping you alive. Relax your right hand, feel your palm getting heavier and warmer. Relax your thumb, index, middle, ring and little finger. Relax your lower arm, your elbow, your upper arm. Imagine your right shoulder's ball and socket. Open it slightly. Feel your whole arm getting warmer and heavier. Relax your left hand, feel it getting warmer and heavier. Relax your left thumb, index, middle, ring and little finger. Relax your left lower arm, your elbow, your left upper arm. See the left ball and socket, and slightly open it. Relax your lower back, your middle back, your upper back. Caress the lumbar and cervical curves on your back. They help you stand upright. Thank your vertebrae. Relax your neck, think about the point where your cranium sits on your top vertebrae. Relax that spot on your neck that holds so much tension. Feel your shoulders let go, you don't need to hold your body up. Relax your mouth, tongue, cheeks, nose. Feel like your eyes are heavy marbles. Relax your right ear and left ear. Relax the space under each ear lobe, first right and then left. Feel your forehead relaxed. Feel your whole body getting warmer and heavier.

This is the archetypal imagery. If you don't do all the relaxation, spend some time slowing down and breathing.

Imagine that you are outside in a place that you have been before. It could be in your backyard, or on a boat in the ocean, or on the beach... Imagine the scene is playing right now in your mind's eye like a movie in present time. Vivify all your senses. What do you see right in front of you, a tree, the mast of a sail, the ocean lapping near you? Notice colors, the green of the trees, the soft white of the clouds. Then reach out and touch something, like the leaves hanging down, or the sand on the beach, or the smooth wood of a beam. What does it feel like? Move in this setting, see what it feels like to walk, which part of your body is moving? Smell. Do you smell the fresh air in the wind, is it full of humidity, does it smell of the earth, or does it have the aroma of a pine tree? What do you hear? A bird, the sound of waves, the wind in the trees? Vivify this. Be there, make it as if it is happening now.

You are feeling okay. Not too happy, not too sad, just okay. There is nothing to do, no one is depending on you. You are just with yourself right now.

Find a spot where it feels okay to sit down and rest for a bit. Imagine that a positive entity is coming to you.

This time you realize it is an archetype coming. An ally is coming who will help you in your goals. Off in the distance you notice either a color or shape, maybe you don't see anything clearly, but you keep looking, keep looking and some details come into focus. Wait and watch. (Give client time here.) Try to notice details. Stay with the visual image, feeling or sense. Think a minute if something comes to mind. Does this remind you of anything you have seen before? An archetype can be a symbol, animal, energy, person, or deity. Hold it for a bit. Let the imagery move if it will. See what the archetype does or says. (Wait a bit more.) Let the imagery complete itself. Is there anything you want to bring forward from the imagery? An image, a feeling? Slowly come back to the here and now.

Step 4: Debrief imagery

Help the client describe the archetype. What does it look like? It can be one from the quiz, or it could be a new one. It can be vague as in a color, or symbolic as in an ocean wave. But in any case, try to get a name for the archetype. Take some time here.

Step 5: Archetype story, homework for next session (written as if talking to a client)

You are going to write a story. Here is a worksheet to use as a guide.

HOMEWORK: ARCHETYPE STORY

1. Name of main character: *(This will be you, but you can give yourself a different name.)*

2. Color associated with character:

3. Test or difficulty of story: *(This will be something similar to the situation from the scenario.)*

4. Helper in story: *(This will be the archetype from the imagery. Think how the archetype can help. But there may be other helpers as well. The archetype can talk to the main character or give gifts or feelings.)*

5. Characteristic: *(What characteristic does the archetype bring?)*

6. What is the end of the story?

Now write a beginning scene using rich sensory detail. Where are you? What's around you? Then continue the story with the character, the test or difficulty, the archetype helper, the main characteristic of the archetype, and then the end. It can be silly, magical or realistic. It can be one page or several. Just do what seems right. Put some colors on the page; draw anything that comes to mind, if you want.

SOME EXAMPLES OF CHARACTERISTICS
Brave, strong, inquisitive, wise, curious, vulnerable, deep, insecure, wounded, loving, caring, creative, musical, afraid, ugly, angry, open, wondering, knowledgeable, foolish, innocent, trusting.

SESSION 3

The purpose of this session is to review the story. If the client sends you the written story, still ask him or her to talk through it. Have an open-ended discussion about the contents of the story and any insights from it. Probe on how the archetype was a helper in the story. Clients are usually motivated to talk about the story in detail and sometimes speculate on what might happen.

If the client doesn't write a story, just stay with his or her process. You can return to earlier session elements, the scenario, feeling and/or goal, or create the story together. Did anything come up again that was similar to the earlier scenario? Does the goal still have energy for him or her? How are they feeling about their archetype? It could be that just talking about the archetype is fine. The main goal is to have an archetype and pinpoint a characteristic that will help with the goal.

SESSION 4

Again stay with the client's process. Check in about the last week. What has been happening with the archetype? Did the story develop any further either in the journal or in spontaneous imagery? Ask again if any event has occurred that gave him or her the feeling from the scenario. Also ask about the goal. If it feels right, you might discuss how to set up a practice with the archetype. Examples would be taking a moment when the client senses the feeling from the scenario, taking a breath and visualizing the archetype.

ADDITIONAL SESSIONS

Schedule as needed. It may be that the individual pace of moving through the steps is taking longer or less time.

FOLLOW-UP

Check in with the client at regular intervals as appropriate for your practice, but at least one follow-up is necessary. See if any current events evoked the same feeling from the scenario. If the helping relationship is continuing, the sequence of the sessions could be cycled through again with a new scenario. Clients may internalize this process over time to apply it for themselves.

CASE STUDIES

TREVOR

Trevor is a 57-year-old counselor living in the Midwest of the U.S. He was a veteran of the U.S. Navy with many years' active duty under his belt and two tours of duty in Afghanistan. He has a master's degree in military psychology and policy and is married with an adult daughter. His interest is networking, empowering and helping vets to transition to new settings, first as a counselor for vets re-entering college, then as a facilitator of various online support environments.

Scenario: Trevor was very active in every setting he found himself in, be it church, graduate school or counselor at a community college. His mission was to help other vets wherever he found them to help make needed transitions. At his graduate school, which was a distributed model combining face-to-face with online environments, he was setting up Internet discussion sites for vets to find support and engage in dialogue. People who were on one site started criticizing him for not being put on another site; some were angry and lashed out. Trevor was surprised, flummoxed and upset. In part he was feeling inadequate to help the vets. He was also upset that vets were expressing anger to solve problems, because it would not help them. He did empathize with the anger at being marginalized by society after risking their lives when they had difficulty getting services or being accepted. We talked for a while about this, and I worked with him to locate the feelings in his body and name them. Trevor was a military officer and being in control and not expressing emotions had been reinforced in him. I noticed through our coaching that Trevor had a bit of resistance to naming emotions he was experiencing. But he had a lot of confidence, and he wouldn't go along with any of my suggestions that didn't feel right. I was pleased at this because it meant that whatever we came up with would be authentic. The best we could do on emotional level was that his hands felt clenched. We talked more and came up with the goal of being able to hold a calm space when helping vets.

Feeling from scenario: As mentioned above, his feeling was clenched fists that showed apprehension. He felt he should be doing something else to help vets—what he was doing wasn't working.

Goal for coaching: Trevor's goal was to "hold a calm space when interacting with vets." He wanted to be able to create a framework for calm space and have a higher level of consciousness hold space.

Archetype from quiz: Since he wanted an emotional goal, I asked him to take the tarot quiz. At first, he thought he would get something like the hero or something similar to a warrior, because of his military background. He mentioned that a lot of working with vets is understanding that they are dealing with a hero-warrior archetype and trying to figure out how to integrate this into their new lives in civilian society. However, after he took the quiz he got the magician and the world, and after more thinking he decided to keep the magician.

Homework, research on archetype: He did Internet research on images and descriptions of the magician. In the images he saw water and noticed that the figure was holding a silver goblet. Further, he reported that the magician acted consciously and mindfully while acknowledging his motivation and intention. Trevor reported that the positive side of magician energy was getting things done. Conversely, the negative side of their work is ego involvement. This made sense to Trevor since he wanted to make things happen for vets He could apply this archetype to his goal of keeping a calm space within. We did the archetype imagery exercises after this discussion.

Archetype from imagery: During the imagery Trevor saw a silver goblet. Trevor liked this a lot because it symbolized creating a holding vessel for the vets. He said his imagery experience had a spiritual dimension. That led Trevor to talk about the idea of a warrior monk. To symbolize this, he held his hands with his wrists together and fingers cupped as in a chalice. I thought it was a lovely synchronicity. His images were giving him the same message.

Story: Trevor wrote a story about an encounter with a warrior-monk and told me about it during a session. He was in a grove of trees by a quiet lake, practicing yoga. In the middle of one of his stretches he saw bands of color that he hadn't seen before. When he stood up he saw a young man dressed in black holding a silver chalice. The young man did not speak but handed him the chalice, and as Trevor looked inside he saw a pale green light. The chalice had the property of rewind. He started to see interactions that started to play like movies, of specific interactions in the past, and he was able to replay these. After a while he realized that he was worrying for no reason. He had been fine in these interactions. When he looked in the chalice he felt calm and confidence. As he was describing this experience, it seemed real to him, not just a story, he was grappling with issues of detachment. But the word didn't seem quite right, it was more like about being present. After looking at the chalice a while, he went back to the lake again, and didn't see the young man, but he had a sense of his energy which he termed the "warrior-monk." He had the feeling that he needed to give the chalice to someone else. He was feeling tired or fatigued at looking at past incidents. He wondered what would be next.

As we talked more, he described his experience of creating the story as lucid dreaming, since he was consciously having visions during the day. In this dream the energy from the chalice became a purple glow. He experienced a flash of lightning in his awareness.

During this session, we then moved to discussing his thoughts on the story, and he brought up Ken Wilber's theories (1996); Wilber is a transpersonal psychologist identified with integral theory. In the theory there are four quadrants to understand any phenomenon: intentional, behavioral, cultural and social. One of the ideas is that sophistical development was conveyed by the letters AQAL, or "all quadrants all levels." Maybe that was what Trevor was experiencing with the purple light.

He also talked about applying the energy of holding space while he was working on analyzing his data from interviews for his dissertation. He was listening to the interviews over and over to open up a quiet space to really listening to what his participants were saying. He seemed to be automatically applying the energy from the archetypal silver chalice in many elements of his life.

Follow-up: At our final session we talked a lot about the chalice and how its glowing light had turned to purple. He seemed to want to give it to someone else. He didn't need it all the time, and he didn't want to need a crutch. We talked a bit about archiving it for when he needed it. Now when he looked into the purple glow he didn't see past things, he saw the present. He saw faces and fractal patterns and pieces of art in a gallery. The message, he said, was to pay attention. He also gave examples of using the purple light in other settings, when he was at a conference and wanted to talk to several people. He evoked the purple light, and surprisingly they ended up coming up to him. The main teaching to him of the chalice with purple light was to pay attention to the way he wanted to be. Instead of being instrumental and making things happen it was a matter of allowing. He felt his work with coaching had helped him be present in a new way.

MAYA

In her early forties, Maya was born in Mexico and moved to the U.S. as a teenager, and now lived in New York. She was a global learning manager for a Fortune 500 multinational. She was married and during the coaching was expecting twins.

Scenario: She thought about a recent time when she was not happy or uncomfortable. She was in a phone meeting with training leaders from Europe and Latin America, rolling out a new online curriculum. They were telling her in a very insistent manner that the new curriculum would not work. All of a sudden Maya felt a feeling of "cold" throughout her body, particularly in her stomach. She felt like she had gone into a black hole that was bottomless. She felt she was not as smart as she was supposed to be, and she was very worried that she would disappoint her boss who had appointed her to this job. Even though she had a masters and an MBA, all of a sudden she felt like she wasn't qualified, and she was vividly afraid of failure.

Feeling from scenario: As noted above, the main feeling was a cold stomach.

Goal for coaching: Her goal was "I choose to self-validate that I am doing a good job."

Archetype from quiz: Magician and Moon.

Homework research on archetype: Maya looked up images and information for both the magician and the moon on the Internet. Her research showed that the magician used the four elements. Also, the magician could take the emotional powers of the soul to change things on a physical basis. In images, his right hand was to heaven and his left hand was to the earth. The magician connected both worlds.

In terms of the moon, her research showed that the card had a dog and a wolf or sometimes a bear. The controlled world was represented by a dog, and the wolf or bear represented the uncontrolled world. There was a crayfish coming out of the water, and in the background were two pillars. As the crayfish came out of the water toward the pillars, it represented to her that her insights were coming from her unconscious. Maya said that the ego holds on to the conscious, but she thought to find peace she needed to open it up. I was happy to hear her say this since it lined up with the models I had shown at the beginning of coaching. She also mentioned ideas from the Myers and Briggs Type Indicator (MBTI) test which she used to coach executives. In this test, water represents the unconscious.

As she was talking about her research on the cards, all of a sudden she thought about letting down her twins. To me this was related to her scenario of being afraid that she would let her boss down, and that she would be wrong. I thought this was positive that some emotional content came out during the session.

Then she continued reporting her research on the archetypes. The moon was white and far away, but the magician was yellow, wrapped up in kindness. It was a warm, hugging light.

We then did the archetypal imagery. Out of the imagery came Yellow Wisdom. It was a warm glow that made her feel safe. After that, she went back to the scenario of being questioned at work in the imagery with the yellow wisdom. She felt safe, the situation now felt completely different.

Archetype from imagery: Maya's archetype from imagery was Yellow Wisdom.

Story: We reviewed her story during a session. She had written it, but I asked her to tell me about it. The story began in her office the day before the event from the scenario when people were questioning her. She noticed a different light in the office than before. Then she wrote about going swimming. She followed the instructions by making the story rich in sensory details and noted her perceptions clearly as well as her feelings. The story moved to the scenario, as she was meeting with the global team about the change in the online curriculum. Although this time, after the Latin American and London colleagues questioned her, "Yellow Wisdom had peeked his head. Radiating the warmth that tended to be part of him, he managed to stop the chill." It had felt weird to be questioned, but Yellow Wisdom forced her to stop and feel. The interaction had felt different because now she had a visceral response. Her whole body was listening. She felt she had new insights; Maya used the phrase "eye opening" in talking about the change in her story. A paraphrase of what she said then was, "I could go through life without thinking, on auto pilot, or I could try to feel things. I can now stop and trust myself." She realized the strength of what she was doing. The chill stopped. Yellow Wisdom became a wise woman. In the discussion, Maya drew a picture of her trust in herself as moving upward, slowing; it went up and down but the trajectory was upward. She expressed again, "I will stop and trust."

At the next session, she shared some writing from her journal. She had spontaneously started writing affirmations. Some of them were the following:

I can always ask for help.

I know! If not I can ask for help.

I am good enough and strong enough.

I don't always have to know.

When I feel cold, I'll be gray. My image is grayed out.

I'm the one to choose to be gray or not.

I don't always have to have the right answer.

She drew images of "how I can trust myself." She had drawn a Buddha-like figure with a yellow glow on top, and trees around it. It was a night-time scene of a park in the city. There was a moon in the background. She also talked about feeling "grayed out," similar to when her stomach was cold. Instead of having this feeling automatically, she wanted to choose when she became gray; for example, she could step back from a situation that was charged.

Follow-up: Eight weeks after coaching began and three weeks after the fourth session, we had a follow-up meeting. When asked how she was doing on her goal she said, "Slightly better." I was a bit concerned. But she reported a subtle shift which seemed very positive to me, since she expressed that the main change was that she is able to catch herself when she is first starting to doubt herself. I reinforced this, since bringing awareness to a non-functional pattern is so important, moving to action instead of reaction. I asked her if she had had any other instances of feeling cold in her stomach or "grayed out" recently. She said not, even when she had given a presentation of a new effort to her boss. She said she now felt she wasn't alone, and didn't have to be right all the time. Yellow Wisdom reminded her that she knew what she knew, and it was okay not to know. We talked about what Yellow Wisdom was. I asked if it was a part of her or not. She struggled with words for a bit. She said it wasn't consciously a part of her. She evoked her Mexican heritage saying that during pre-colonial times, there was a concept of *nahual*, or a guardian animal. I asked if it was similar to a shamanic power animal, and she said yes. She didn't want to set up a practice with Yellow Wisdom, but wanted to keep in mind that he was always there. The work felt complete. I asked her to email if the cold feeling came back.

I asked for feedback on the sessions. She said it was unlike other coaching she had done, since it was holistic with the imagery and the archetypes.

NAPUA

Scenario: Napua chose this pseudo name for herself, which means many flowers or children in Hawaiian. She started the session by saying she often sat and spaced out. She felt like she didn't know how to take care of herself. She had told her boss that she couldn't keep up the work. She felt she just couldn't take care of herself. Her husband had just died, after she had been taking care of him for three years. She was seeing a psychiatrist and was diagnosed with chronic depression. As part of this condition, she wasn't sleeping well. She consistently thought, "I have to be better and work harder." There was always a feeling of anger at herself. She felt as a scornful mother to herself, always criticizing. This was true even though she was very successful with a master's degree and worked as a community organizer and college teacher. Instead of talking about a specific event, we spent quite a bit of time discussing her feelings. Out of this she created the following goal. It was almost like she needed relief from a constant state of distress. She needed help escaping feeling bad about herself.

Goal for coaching: This was Napua's goal: "I want to be accepting of myself. I want to relax and be with myself."

Archetype from quiz: She had decided to take the archetype quiz, and had an interesting approach. Napua took the test three times. First she took it with no goal in mind, then she took it with "what is now?" and finally she took it a third time with "how I want to be." She had a number of different archetypes which came up, but strength came up all three times.

Archetype from imagery: During the next session, we talked about the archetype of strength. Then, we did the archetypal imagery. In this imagery she was in her backyard sitting by a tree, and her dog came to her. This dog had died in the recent past. His name was Hush Puppy, and he put his head on her lap and said, "Everything is going to be okay." Hush Puppy was a red pit bull. When he was alive he'd been a loving watch dog who protected her. She said she felt better and calmer after the imagery. We reviewed her feelings of inadequacies and being "spaced out" all the time. She affirmed that everything was okay now since Hush Puppy told her everything was okay. She said, "I love myself. I have lots in my heart." She then brought up the ocean, which is a big part of her life in Hawaii. To her the ocean was strength and full of healing.

Follow-up: At the next session, Napua talked about her grief for her husband's death, which had happened six months earlier. She said she hadn't given herself time to grieve. Hush Puppy came up again. He would come when she needed him, and she wouldn't feel afraid. Whenever she is afraid, Hush Puppy would be there; he didn't want her to beat herself up. She then moved on to the idea of needing to be weak to be strong. Napua had decided to withdraw from her graduate program, which seemed to be a relief since she was removing pressure. She would restart when she felt more centered. She had also broken her fibula during the coaching sessions, and was framing this as a test. She was learning to accept herself more, and didn't need to prove herself. She could ask for help. We did another imagery session, and Hush Puppy came to her, as well as her living dogs Kamole, which meant Earth, and Kaao, which meant Sun. They said to her, "Let's go to the beach." To her this meant to go to the water to cleanse and to heal. She liked the coaching sessions since she rarely talked to anyone about how she was feeling. She was feeling better.

Summary: Key coaching elements from case studies

Key coaching elements	Trevor	Maya	Napua
Demographics	Male, 57, retired Navy officer, counselor for vets returning to college	Female, 42, born in Latin America, lives in New York City, an executive for a Fortune 500 multinational	Female, in her fifties, native Hawaiian, teaches at a community college
Scenario	He was setting up Internet support sites for vets and was criticized	She was presenting a new training curriculum to global trainers, and they questioned it	She felt spaced out all the time, and didn't know how to take care of herself. Her husband had just died
Feeling from scenario	Clenching hands	Cold in the stomach	Helplessness
Goal for coaching	I want to be a calm presence when working with vets	I choose to self-validate that I'm doing a good job	I want to be accepting of myself
Archetype from quiz	Magician	Magician and Moon	Strength
Archetype from imagery	Silver Chalice radiating a pale green light	Yellow Wisdom	Hush Puppy (a red pit bull)
Characteristics	Allows him to see interactions and replay them so he is calm	Creates warmth	Reassurance

Worksheet: Key coaching points

Key coaching points	
Scenario	
Feeling from scenario	
Goal for coaching	
Archetype from quiz	
Archetype from imagery	
Characteristics	

CHAPTER 9

WHAT IF LIFE WERE SWEET?

My dad was dying of stomach cancer, and it had metastasized to his bones. He was in the process of bleeding to death internally, since the tumors were secreting toxins that would ruin the pH balance. His blood vessels could no longer keep their shape. I said, "Dad, are you afraid?" He said, "No, life is sweet." I admired my dad's courage and wanted to be like him, to experience life in its sweetness. If each of us takes on the task of becoming wise, this action will, in effect, change human interaction so that life is sweet for many. Transforming the mind to wisdom can fill it with a gentle wind. There is a natural flow from the energy field to conscious awareness.

As more people transform, then it could start a cascading effect paving the way for others. English biologist Rupert Sheldrake (1995) called the energy field the "morphogenetic field." His hypothesis was that when animals and humans learn new actions or information, these new patterns are fed into this space. Once it resides there, then others with similar genetics can pick up the information more quickly. This may seem illogical to some, but to me it has some face validity. The more people who learn something new, the easier it seems for other people to pick it up. For example, think about when a new sport is introduced, like snowboarding. Initially very few people do it, but over time it seems easier and easier for people to learn. Supporting Sheldrake's ideas, Ken Wilber (1996), a popular spiritual teacher, posits the evolution of consciousness, explaining that as more people move into their spirituality then human consciousness will actually change in that direction for others. As human consciousness changes, energy patterns that motivate human actions, or archetypes, transform as well. A case in point is that masculine and feminine archetypes are combining to prompt people to become more whole.

Marion Woodman (Woodman and Dickson 1996), a psychologist, in her book *Dancing in the Flames* looks at human evolution in broad strokes by describing a paradigm shift in human consciousness during contemporary times. The words "paradigm shift" have become trendy and trite, but I think that Woodman uses the phrase in a meaningful way to explain major changes in the underlying assumptions of how society works. In ancient times humans had a matriarchal paradigm as described in *The Chalice and the Blade* by Riane Eisler (1988). The main source of power was the feminine, since agriculture was of primary importance. During this time, women's ability to give birth and grow plants was the source of control and power. People valued women, and the ability to create life was venerated. Over time as societies developed, the patriarchy established order to accomplish tasks for a civil society. People who were authoritarian were privileged in society. According to Woodman, humans have evolved so that generating life and establishing control are both needed. This creates wholeness combining both dualities. Both modes are needed, and people can incorporate both feminine and masculine qualities. Woodman called this new paradigm androgyny, where humans have power from both female and male assets. If society has moved from matriarchy to patriarchy and is now combining them for androgyny, then these two opposites are being balanced. There is fluidity between control and generativity depending on the need, and the opposites inform each other.

Figure 9.1 The androgyny paradigm includes both matriarchy and patriarchy. A wise mind has room for both

THE WISE MIND

Taking on the task to create a wise mind can have many benefits for the individual person and possibly also help the collective. If the evolution of consciousness is correct, then this transformation spreads from the individual to the whole. Creating a spacious wise mind isn't really opening up the Tao so the polarities are blended or are creating homogeneity. Rather, the barrier to the unconscious becomes permeable so that awareness is open. As individual humans pursue a course that leads to a wise mind, opposites are tolerated and can be adapted at will as they are needed. A wise mind is spacious, giving awareness room to open the unconscious. This in turn creates many benefits including health, creativity, problem-solving ability, enhanced spirituality and a holistic view of humans' connection to the Earth.

Figure 9.2 The wise mind is spacious as awareness is open to the unconscious

What follows are a few tidbits of how creating a spacious mind allows the opposites to coexist for health, creativity, problem-solving, logic, spirituality and human and ecological balance.

HEALTH BENEFITS

A person who has opened the mind has increased physical health. As a matter of fact, immune responses can improve. The task of creating a wise mind by finding an archetype and visualizing it will improve imagery skills. Learning to create vivid mental images prompts relaxation. The heart rate goes down, as does blood pressure. Imagery magically travels through the unconscious barrier and talks to the autonomic nervous system, particularly the part that restores the body. The two parts are the sympathetic nervous system and the parasympathetic nervous system. The first system rouses all the senses and dumps adrenaline into the system for the fight-or-flight response, and the second one restores, relaxes and improves immune activity. Seeing oneself floating in a warm, turquoise pool of water of water gives the parasympathetic system the signal to do its job and turns off the sympathetic. Since the two parts of the autonomic nervous system are inversely related, when one is activated the other shuts down. When the parasympathetic is active through images, the body can rest and restore with imagery, as the opposite response of stimulation shuts down. Stress that can contribute to illness can be pacified. Opening the mind allows a person to activate the parasympathetic or sympathetic nervous system as needed.

Figure 9.3 A spacious mind lets either the PNS restore
for healing or the SNS activate to get things done

CREATIVITY AND PROBLEM SOLVING

A wise mind also increases creativity and problem-solving ability. Opening the unconscious creates the mental space for open-ended or divergent thinking, which stimulates creativity. With this mode, dissimilar and unconnected ideas can come into the mind even though they don't seem to make sense at a given time. Convergent thinking is the opposite mental action, where ideas are focused in a linear format, one concept at a time.

Figure 9.4 Divergent thinking opens the mind, and convergent thinking
focuses the mind. Both are needed in creativity and problem solving.
The spacious mind gives space for both types of thinking

Another way to look at the two modes of thinking in the creative process is to use the words intuition and logic, instead of divergent and convergent. In the creative process, the intuitive and rational are intertwined. The intuitive can be equated with divergent and imagistic thinking as the mind entertains many subtleties at once, while the rational is similar to convergent thinking as it focuses on one idea at a time in a logical order.

The wise mind is spacious, allowing opposites to coexist. When logic is needed it can come to the foreground while intuition is in the background, or vice versa. Awareness keeps the space open for the interplay to happen.

The creative process has a number of steps which use both intuition and logic. First, the rational delineates a problem, and then there is a waiting period called incubation. During this phase intuition is active. Insights pop into the mind. Often in business settings, team leaders use a brainstorming experience, where people express ideas no matter how silly or unrelated. This prompts divergence. Facilitators sometimes say that the best ideas don't come until the group is tired and people have stopped trying. The unconscious opens to produce ideas. After incubation, an insight comes, sometimes in a vision. The scientist who made the discovery that nerves act to move muscles with electrical stimuli was sitting in front of a fire in a dream state and visualized an experiment needed to prove this. After the insight, logic and the rational mind kick in to verify the creative solution. Learning to image and opening the unconscious lets the whole mind breathe creativity into the human condition.

A wise mind is not only better at creativity but also better at logic. It seems counterintuitive, since people are usually defined as creative or logical, but creating space in the mind allows the opposites their play.

Figure 9.5 Intuition and logic are both needed for creativity, and the spacious mind has room for both

LOGIC AND EMOTIONS

Fear and emotions are the enemy of logic since they constrict and skew perceptions. Often people are nervous when giving a public speech. They don't notice what is going on around. It is hard to think clearly, let alone logically. With the opening of the unconscious, there are no hidden emotions that exaggerate day-to-day experiences. There is softness to the inner world which lets emotions come and go. Spaciousness lets the mind do its work of sorting out problems, seeing connections and reflecting on possibilities.

Figure 9.6 Suppressed emotions can constrict the mind so that logic cannot flow. The wise mind gives space for this to happen

SPIRITUALITY

Enhancing health and all kinds of thinking is a benefit of the wise mind, but a further benefit is spirituality. Some spiritual sages teach that overcoming the human condition is a prerequisite. Their message is that humanity is at odds to higher enlightenment. Further, they say that to become spiritual people need to control the physical being in all its base desires. Freud's view of the unconscious as the seat of sexual motivation was in this line of thinking. But if humans develop a wise mind, the instinctual elements can be put in their place by enhanced awareness. As the unconscious opens, the spirit Self transmits insights for the greater good.

Figure 9.7 The path to wisdom is finding the spirit Self residing deep in the unconscious. It is an inward journey through the body, so that the physical and spiritual are balanced

HUMANS AND ECOLOGICAL BALANCE

Wisdom comes from the realization of spirit in matter. Sophia is the creator in the Dead Sea Scrolls and this text records that matter sprang out of her being and then subdivided in the exponential diversity of life. Sophia represents the journey of finding spirit in matter, not in spite of it. An analog to the individual quest for spirituality is to open the mind to become wise.

The wise mind concept foreshadows a reality where there is not a division between mind and spirit, but humanity and spirituality are the same. Wise people see the big picture of the interconnection of all of life and can act for the benefit of the whole.

The Earth is in distress. The arctic ice cap is melting and the number of species threatened with extinction grows daily. What is needed now is a sea change of human awareness to sustain life on the Earth. People who have transformed toward wisdom can perceive the changes that need to be made to sustain life. The matriarchy was about generating life, and the patriarchy was about controlling human systems to create order and stability. Humanity needs both right now, the ability to generate life as well as the skills to control human activity to sustain life.

Figure 9.8 Wisdom can translate to a greater awareness of humans' place in the Earth's ecosystem to sustain life in all its form

The possibility of a person becoming wise translates to understanding and adapting to humans' connection to the Earth. Woodman's androgynous paradigm is marked by a keen awareness of the interconnection of life. With wisdom, human actions can be analyzed with creativity and logic for sustainability. Human patterns can be controlled to support life on Earth. If an action would destroy ecosystems, reduce oxygen for animals or carbon dioxide for plants, it would not be supported.

ARCHETYPES FOR TRANSFORMATION

Opening the mind to wisdom is not an easy task. It is a complex and simultaneously subtle endeavor. The ego's hold on stability is sacrificed for the connection to spirit that brings peace and joy. The delusion of control and separation erodes to a softer, warmer and friendlier awareness. The sense of Self is not constricted to fragmented thoughts or overwhelming emotions. Trust doesn't rest with control of the inner world, but with the sense of interconnection. Stability comes from a focus of attention, not from a defensive posture.

There is a theme in both the deity and tarot archetypes. Almost all of them face a crisis. Lilith is thrown out of Eden. Isis' husband is taken and murdered. Avalokiteshvara loses his faith and his brain is shattered, while Ganesha's head is cut off. These deities became powerful in the face of despair, pain, grief and rejection. The world they inhabited ended in some way, and survival depended on adaptation to tap the power inside to become wise. The unconscious not only contained their fears, but also hid their strengths. When the unconscious is opened, hidden strengths are apparent. An individual is essentially changed from the inside out since there is more energy and power.

Transformation is a common quality of major tarot archetypes as well. With Judgment a new day is dawning. With the World, dreams have been fulfilled. Justice prompts wrongs to be righted, as an injustice is settled. The Hanged Man allows a release of what has been past. The old life has changed, and the present is made new.

Identifying with archetypes helps a person go through these same transformations in the inner world to become wise and sustain the experience of peace and joy. I urge all of us to accept the wisdom challenge for a future that is spacious in wisdom to realize our potential. We could create joy and peace, not just for ourselves but for life on the planet as well. If there are many wise minds, life could truly become sweet for many.

APPENDIX 1

TAROT ARCHETYPE QUIZ

The quiz below is to help your intuition be the guide to an archetype from the tarot. Read through these statements. Check seven of the statements that most closely fit how you would describe yourself. After marking the seven statements, look at the number in parenthesis and mark that number in the following archetype quiz key. For example, if you choose "I feel things before they happen," you will have marked #1 in the archetype quiz key. You will then have selected a few archetypes. Then look them up in Chapter 6 and see which one strikes your fancy.

Check seven (7) that best describe you.

☐ I feel things before they happen. (#1)

☐ It feels like a new day. (#20)

☐ I am able to right wrongs. (#8)

☐ I can get the financial and legal resources I need. (#4)

☐ I feel equilibrium, like I hang out in the middle of the Tao, straddling yin and yang. (#14)

☐ Things are going my way. (#3)

☐ I feel deeply connected to spirit. (#5)

☐ I feel passionate and joyful. (#6)

☐ A painful event has happened. (#13)

☐ People often ask for my advice. (#2)

- ❑ I have great luck. (#10)
- ❑ I need time to reflect by myself. (#9)
- ❑ I can feel a change coming on, but I am not sure how it will manifest. (#18)
- ❑ I feel great because the Sun is out. (#19)
- ❑ The old has died. (#20)
- ❑ I am very playful. (#0)
- ❑ I often have a dream or a body sense about something that is about to happen. (#1)
- ❑ I feel isolated. (#9)
- ❑ I am able to get things done. (#11)
- ❑ I release myself to the universe. #(12)
- ❑ People see me as successful. (#7)
- ❑ I often feel ecstasy. (#6)
- ❑ I often feel in an unreal dream state. (#15)
- ❑ There is a sudden change in how my life is working. (#16)
- ❑ I am experiencing a quiet time to heal. (#17)
- ❑ Something that I really wanted has happened. (#21)
- ❑ I feel spontaneous and innocent. (#0)
- ❑ I seem to understand the big picture and have a deep perspective of events. (#2)
- ❑ I feel integrated emotionally, physically, mentally and spiritually. (#21)
- ❑ I seem to attract money. (#3)
- ❑ I am very happy. (#19)
- ❑ I easily find myself as a leader in organizations. (#4)
- ❑ I feel attuned to psychic energy. (#18)

❑ People say I radiate good energy. #(5)

❑ I feel that I am receiving spiritual energy for my betterment. (#17)

❑ I am getting what I want. (#7)

❑ Balance has been restored and justice achieved. (#8)

❑ The way things were is over, and there is a new order. (#15)

❑ I live my life with not too much and not too little. (#14)

❑ There will be a turn for the better in my life. (#10).

❑ I feel empty inside. (#13)

❑ I feel very empowered like I can do anything. (#11)

❑ I have freely and completely let go of the old ways. (#12)

❑ The old ways are breaking up. #(16)

TAROT ARCHETYPE QUIZ KEY

Mark a check beside each archetype from the seven you chose in the Archetype Quiz. Pay attention to the archetypes that you have checked more than once.

❑ #0 Fool Innocence

❑ #1 Magician Intuition

❑ #2 High Priestess Wisdom

❑ #3 Empress Abundance

❑ #4 Emperor Authority

❑ #5 Hierophant Spirituality

❑ #6 Lovers Union

❑ #7 Chariot Success

❑ #8 Justice Balance

❑ #9 Hermit Solitude

❑ #10 Wheel of Fortune Luck

❑ #11 Strength Prowess

❑ #12 Hanged Man Surrender

❑ #13 Death Loss

❑ #14 Temperance Moderation

❑ #15 Devil Delusion

❑ #16 Tower Disruption

❑ #17 Star Healing

❑ #18 Moon Unconscious

❑ #19 Sun Happiness

❑ #20 Judgment Renewal

❑ #21 World Fulfillment

Match the archetype numbers with the descriptions in Chapter 6. If you get the same number twice, that might be your archetype. If not, you can look at the major arcana archetypes in that chapter, matching the numbers to the ones you picked. Pick one that seems right to you. Amplify your encounter with one by finding it on the web, or find pictures, poems or stories about it in books. Read about the archetype in as many places as possible, draw a picture, write in a journal, compose a poem or create a collage. Find music that reminds you of its characteristics, and follow your intuition. Stay with an archetype as long as it feels right. Besides using this quiz to find a major arcana archetype, you can also use a deck. You can look at decks in New Age stores, and buy one that feels right. I recommend getting a deck with the structure of 4 suits and 22 majors. Then the 22 can be pulled out separately, these cards shuffled, and one pulled as an experiment to find an archetype for potential fascination.

DEITY ARCHETYPE QUIZ

Use this survey to select one of the five archetypes presented in Chapter 7. Circle the number of the top five statements that you consider matches most closely your personality. Note the number of those questions in the boxes following the quiz. Use the answer key to find your archetype.

1. I stand up to authority.
2. I have many faces.
3. I would do anything to protect life.
4. I have special gifts.
5. I am often drawn to help others.
6. When I am with a group I can feel the energy of the group.
7. I put myself out to help others.
8. Someone has inflicted a terrible blow to me.
9. I am innovative.
10. I have sacrificed to help a purpose greater than myself.
11. I feel others use me to get what they want.
12. My life's aspiration is to be spiritual.
13. I feel deeply connected to the Earth.
14. I feel misunderstood.

15. I consider myself powerful.

16. I have worked hard in my life.

17. I have had someone deliver a mortal wound to me.

18. People look up to me.

19. I have a strong animal nature.

20. I am really strong.

21. I feel I've had a major transformation in my life.

22. People seem to give me things.

23. I have put myself out to help someone.

24. I feel beautiful.

25. I am extremely creative.

Write the numbers below of your answers.

DEITY ARCHETYPE QUIZ KEY

If you have two or more that match an archetype below, read about her or him in Chapter 7 and see if you might like to choose that archetype to work with for a while:

Lilith (Brave): 1, 9, 13, 14, 19

Isis (Generator): 4, 8, 10, 18, 24

Gaia (Protector): 3, 7, 11, 15, 25

Ganesha (Generous): 5, 17, 20, 22, 23

Avalokiteshvara (Compassion): 2, 6, 12, 16, 21

APPENDIX 3

TAROT READING BASICS

As noted in Chapter 6, the tarot is a deck of 78 cards used for divination. It appeared in Northern Italy in the fifteenth century, based on a card game that came from Egypt. There are four suits like the current play deck which has hearts, diamonds, clubs and spades. The four suits in tarot differ depending on the deck, but the following are often used: wands, pentacles, swords and cups. Unlike the play deck, which only has one card without a suit, the joker, the tarot has 22 cards with no suits. These are termed the major arcana with no suits and are numbered 0–21. I recommend getting a deck with the traditional organization of four suits and 22 majors. There are many revisionist decks that don't use this structure, but the reading basics below rely on a traditional tarot structure.

I think it is important to think about what tarot cards or other divination tools actually tell readers. Most people who ask to get their cards read usually want to know about love affairs or money. Some expect to get specific factual answers. However, I think that the answers are trends, not facts. By this I mean a reading can tell which way the energy is moving. It is good to remember that intuition is a sense, and as such it can feel things, but it can't provide what is usually thought to be specifics of right or wrong. Also metaphoric knowledge, as in tarot, is non-rational in nature. It can carry many meanings, and it is filtered through an individual's psychology. Non-rational is not the same as irrational. Irrational answers are usually wrong, but non-rational come from a place of imagery, metaphor, visions or story. It is a way of knowing that may take a process to understand, and can have multiple meanings. It is best to treat tarot with an attitude of "tolerating ambiguity." The answers can be right or wrong. One can learn to trust the body sense, and wait for intuition to present insights. Tarot is a tool to see which direction the wind may be blowing.

People read the tarot by asking a question and then shuffling the deck, cutting and dealing into one of the many prescribed layouts. Each card represents certain energy, and the placement of the card has a given meaning. The tarot is a system of knowing which is cyclic in nature. The suits start at the ace and go to a face card. When one gets to the top face card such as a king, then the cycle is ready to begin again with an ace. Similarly, the majors start at 0 and go to 21. Number 21, the world, is the ultimate fulfillment card, but this is close as well to 0, or the innocence needed to start all over.

My favorite layout is the Celtic Cross, since it is relatively quick and gives some comprehensive perspective at the same time. First formulate a question. This can be general, one like "What is going on with Annabelle right now?", or it can be very specific including a time frame as in "Will I get a $5000 raise next January?" I like to get the question clear before I start shuffling. After shuffling the cards well, and cutting them as many times as feels right, lay them out in the order depicted in Figure A3.1. Then go back and look at the position of the cards and interpret each one based on the energy of the suit, number or major in relationship to the place the card holds. For example, the first one is the unconscious position, which means that energy is moving but hasn't manifested yet. Next, look at the card and determine if it is a minor (has a suit) or is a major (has no suit). If it is a major, it has a stronger meaning. Then look up in the table the basic meaning of the card. Here is an example. The two of swords was dealt in the unconscious position. For a minor card, one reads both the number, for example two is balance, and the suit, swords is the mind. Using these interpretations, the card means balance of the mind about forces moving in the unconscious. I would see that this is positive, in that one is not trying to figure things out, but keeping the mind balanced and waiting for changes to manifest. I read reverse cards as the opposite of the upright energy, so if the two of swords is reversed it would be interpreted that the mind is not balancing.

A reader can use intuition in many other ways too. One can see if there are a number of cards with the same suit. This could signify that that type of energy, cups for example or feelings, is playing a large role in someone's life. Also notable could be a number or a face card appearing more than once. One can see how many majors there are, which could indicate that something big is about to appear. Some readers don't use a system like I do, which relies on the symbology of numbers; others read by the pictures on cards. A playful attitude fosters intuition, so think outside the box and have fun while developing a unique style to read tarot.

Figure A3.1 This is the Celtic Cross layout, which is easy to use

ENERGY OF SUITS

Suits can be different but there are always four with energies like those listed below. Most decks come with a little booklet, and this gives information on the four suits. This information can be used when reading a card in thinking about what energy a suit carries:

Wands: Energy

Swords: Mind

Disks/Pentacles: Material things

Cups: Emotions

ENERGY OF MINOR OR SUIT CARDS

Different suits have different face cards, so a reader may need to interpolate the meaning of the cards. There are some feminist decks without ranks. For example, they would have a man, woman and child. One can use the energy of the King and Queen and Page for that.

Number of card or face value	Energy
1	Gift
2	Balance
3	Synthesis
4	Balance
5	Conflict
6	Ecstasy
7	Struggle
8	Stability
9	Coming to Closure
10	Completion
Page	Innocence
Knight	Young Male Energy
Queen	Sophisticated Female Energy
King	Sophisticated Male Energy

ENERGY OF MAJOR CARDS (NO SUITS)

These cards carry more definitive energy. Each one signifies an important force in a person's life.

#0 Fool	Innocence
#1 Magician	Intuition
#2 High Priestess	Wisdom
#3 Empress	Abundance
#4 Emperor	Authority
#5 Hierophant	Spirituality
#6 Lovers	Union
#7 Chariot	Success
#8 Justice	Balance
#9 Hermit	Solitude
#10 Wheel of Fortune	Luck
#11 Strength	Prowess
#12 Hanged Man	Surrender
#13 Death	Loss
#14 Temperance	Moderation
#15 Devil	Delusion
#16 Tower	Disruption
#17 Star	Healing
#18 Moon	Unconscious
#19 Sun	Happiness
#20 Judgment	Renewal
#21 World	Fulfillment

REFERENCES

Achterberg, J. (1985) *Shamanism and Modern Medicine*. Boston and London: Shambhala.

Adler, A. (2009) *Understanding Human Nature: The Psychology of Personality*. London: Oneworld.

Aquinas, T. (1923) *Summa Contra Gentiles*. London: Burns Oates & Washbourne.

Aranya, Swami H. (1963) *Yoga Philosophy of Patanjali* (P.N. Mukerji, Trans.). Calcutta, India: University of Calcutta.

Baring, A. and Cashford, J. (1993) *The Myth of the Goddess: Evolution of an Image*. London: Arkana Penguin.

Bergsma, A. and Ardelt, M. (2012) "Self-reported wisdom and happiness: an empirical investigation." *Journal of Happiness Studies 13*, 481–499.

Bolen, J.S. (2004) *Goddesses in Everywoman: Powerful Archetypes in Women's Lives*. New York, NY: Harper Paperbacks.

Byrne, R. (2006) *The Secret*. Hillsboro, OR: Atria Books/Beyond Words.

Cady, S., Ronanad, M. and Taussig, H. (1986) *Sophia: The Future of Feminist Spirituality*. San Francisco, CA: Harper and Row.

Csikszentmihalyi, M. and Nakamura, J. (2005) "The Role of Emotions in the Development of Wisdom." In R.J. Sternberg and J. Jordan (eds) *A Handbook of Wisdom: Psychological Perspectives*. New York, NY: Cambridge University Press.

Dalai Lama, Tsong-ka-pa and Hopkins, J. (1977) *Tantra in Tibet*. Ithaca, NY: Snow Lion.

Dass, R. (1974) *The Only Dance There Is*. New York, NY: Anchor.

Dass, R. (1979) *Grist for the Mill*. New York, NY: Bantam.

Eisler, R. (1988) *The Chalice and the Blade: Our History, Our Future*. New York, NY: HarperOne.

Erikson, E.H. (1994) *Identity and the Life Cycle,* New York, NY: W.W. Norton.

Freely, J. (1998) *Istanbul: The Imperial City*. London: Penguin.

Freud, S. (1949) *An Outline of Psycho-Analysis*. New York, NY: W.W. Norton.

Gaarder, J. and Moller, P. (2007) *Sophie's World: A Novel About the History of Philosophy*. New York, NY: Farrar, Straus and Giroux.

Gawain, S. (2002) *Creative Visualization: Use the Power of Your Imagination to Create what You Want in your Life*. Novato, CA. New World Library.

Godwin, M. (1990) *Angels: An Endangered Species.* New York, NY: Simon and Schuster.

Green, A.M. (1975) "Biofeedback: Research and Therapy." In N.O. Jacobson (ed.) *New Ways to Health.* Stockholm: Natur ock Kultur.

Grimes, J.A. (1995) *Ganapati, Song of the Self.* Albany, NY: State University of New York Press.

Grof, S. (1989) *Spiritual Emergency* (New Consciousness Reader). Los Angeles: Jeremy Tarcher.

Houston, J. (1997) *The Possible Human: A Course in Enhancing Your Physical, Mental and Creative Abilities.* New York: Jeremy Tarcher.

Houston, J. (2000) "Myths of the future." *The Humanistic Psychologist 28,* 43–58.

Jung, C.G. (1964) *Man and His Symbols.* Garden City, NY: Doubleday.

Jung, C.G. (1970) *Analytical Psychology: Its Theory and Practice.* New York: Vintage.

Kegan, R. (1982) *The Evolving Self: Problem and Process in Human Development.* Cambridge, MA: Harvard University Press.

Kegan, R. (1998) *In Over Our Heads: The Mental Demands of Modern Life.* Cambridge, MA: Harvard University Press.

Lancaster, B.L. and Palframan, J.T. (2009) "Coping with major life events: the role of spirituality and self-transformation." *Mental Health, Religion & Culture 12,* 3, 257–276.

Lao Tzu and Legge, J. (2012) *Tao Te Ching.* Hollywood, FL: Simon & Brown.

Long, J.S. (2000) "The Prism Self: Multiplicity on the Path to Transcendence." In Y. Eisendrat (ed.) *The Psychology of Mature Spirituality.* New York, NY: Routledge.

Loori, J.D. (2008) *Mountain Record of Zen Talks.* Boston and London: Shambhala.

Macy, J. (1991) *World as Lover, World as Self.* Berkeley, CA: Parallax.

Maslow, A. (1970) *Motivation and Personality.* New York, NY: Harper and Row.

Masui, T. (1987) *The Patient's Efforts and Psychotherapy: The Images of Symptoms.* Presented at the 3rd International Imagery Conference, Fukuoka, Japan.

Nelson, A. (1991) "The role of imagery training on Tohono O'odham children's creativity scores." *Journal of American Indian Education,* May, 24–32.

Nelson, A. (1993) *Living the Wheel: Working with Emotions, Terror and Bliss with Imagery.* York Beach, Maine: Samuel Weiser.

Nelson, A. (2007) "The spacious mind: using archetypes for transformation towards wisdom." *The Humanistic Psychologist 35,* 235–246.

Olson, C. (ed.) (1994) *The Book of the Goddess Past and Present.* New York, NY: Cross Road.

Perls, F.S. (1992) *Gestalt Therapy Verbatim.* Gouldsboro, ME: Gestalt Journal Press.

Pert, C.B. (1997) *Molecules of Emotion.* New York, NY: Simon and Schuster.

Post, B.C. and Wade, N.G. (2009) "Religion and spirituality in psychotherapy: a practice-friendly review of research." *Journal of Clinical Psychology 65,* 2, 131–146.

Prabhu, H.R.A. and Bhat, P.S. (2013) "Mind and consciousness in yoga - Vedanta: A comparative analysis with western psychological concepts." *Indian Journal of Psychiatry* 55, 6, 182–186.

Pribram, K.H. (1981) *Language of the Brain: Experimental Paradoxes and Principles in Neuropsychology.* New York, NY: Brandon House.

Rama, S., Ballentine, R. and Ajanja, S. (1976) *Yoga and Psychotherapy: The Evolution of Consciousness.* Honesdale, PA: Himalayan International.

Ray, A.R. (2001) *Secret of the Vajra World: Tantric Buddhism of Tibet.* Boston and London: Shambhala.

Restak, R. (2010) *Think Smart: A Neuroscientist's Prescription for Improving Your Brain's Performance.* New York, NY: Riverhead Trade.

Rogers, C. (1961) *On Becoming a Person: A Therapist's View of Psychotherapy.* New York, NY: Merrill.

Satchidananda, S. (2012) *The Yoga Sutras of Patanjali.* Buckingham, VA: Integral Yoga.

Saxe, J.G. (1963) *The Blind Men and the Elephant; John Godfrey Saxe's Version of the Famous Indian Legend.* New York, NY: Whittlesey House.

Seligman, M.E.P. (2002) *Authentic Happiness.* New York, NY: Free Press.

Sheldrake, R. (1995) *The Hypothesis of a New Science of Life: Morphic Resonance.* Rochester, VT: Park Street.

Soloviev, V. (1978) *Sophia.* Lausanne: L'Age d'Homme.

Tenzin Gyatso, His Holiness (1982) *Essence of Refined Gold.* New York, NY: Snow Lion.

Trungpa, C. (1991) *The Heart of the Buddha.* Boston and London: Shambhala.

Vivekananda, S. (1956) *Raja Yoga.* New York, NY: Ramakrishna-Vivekananda Center.

von Franz, M.-L. (1985) *Aurora Consurgens.* Princeton, NJ: Princeton University Press.

Walsh, R. (2011) "The varieties of wisdom: cross-cultural, and integral contributions." *Research in Human Development* 8, 2, 109–127.

Walters, F. (1977) *The Book of the Hopi.* New York, NY: Penguin.

Watts, A.W. (1999) *The Way of Zen.* New York, NY: Vintage.

Wilber, K. (1996) *A Brief History of Everything.* Boston and London: Shambhala.

Wise, A. (1995) *The High-Performance Mind: Mastering Brainwaves for Insight, Healing and Creativity.* New York, NY: Jeremy Tarcher/Putman.

Woodman, M. and Dickson, E. (1996) *Dancing in the Flames: The Dark Goddess in Personal Transformation.* Boston and London: Shambhala.

Yeshe, L.T. and Ribush, N. (2004) *Becoming Vajrasattva: The Tantric Path of Purification.* Somerville, MA: Wisdom.

Yogananda, P. (2005) *Autobiography of a Yogi.* Nevada City, CA: Crystal Clarity.

SUBJECT INDEX

AUTHOR INDEX